# DOMESTIC ABUSE BREAKTHROUGH FORMULA

## YOUR STEP BY STEP GUIDE TO CREATING A LIFE OF EMOTIONAL FREEDOM FOR YOU AND YOUR FAMILY

### KATE BEESLEY

authors
AND CO.

Disclaimer:

*In places this book contains information derived from memoirs. It reflects the author's present recollections of experiences over time. Some names and characteristics have been changed, some events have been compressed, and some dialogue has been recreated.*

Copyright © 2021 by Kate Beesley

ISBN13: 9798769482182

# DEDICATION

*I dedicate this book to my daughter Sofia.*

*I want you to know just how proud I am of you.*

*My mission is to find purpose from our darkest days.*

*Supporting other women to go from being afraid and overwhelmed to healed and thriving is my legacy to you my beautiful girl.*

*I will nurture this legacy to remind you never allow anyone to dim your light.*

*Continue to shine like the bright star you are and never stop being you.*

*You gave me strength on some of my darkest days and you motivate me everyday to make our dreams a reality.*

*Our bond is like glue.*

*Mummy loves you always. xx*

# CONTENTS

# INTRODUCTION

Having both lived through the effects of domestic abuse personally, and since advancing my skills professionally to specialise specifically in childhood trauma and narcissistic abuse,

I've written this book with you and your healing journey in mind, because I want you, as I have, to break free from the shackles of abuse, so you can start to live the life you are truly meant for; a life filled with happiness and contentment.

There's no denying being in an abusive relationship is soul-destroying, and if your abuser has narcissistic traits then this can make you doubt your own perception on reality, which makes it much harder to break the trauma bond.

Like many little girls, growing up I dreamt of the fairy-tale wedding, marrying my knight in shining armour who had my back no matter what life threw at us.

We all know the script in the vows... In sickness and in health... richer or poorer... Abuse and fear were never part of the deal.

But I was drawn into a fantasy, and it turned out to be just that. The reality was, I felt trapped in a nightmare and I couldn't see any way out.

The relationship started off appearing to be picture perfect, everything I'd always dreamt of, but slowly the cracks began to show and before I knew it, I was a new mum, trapped in a cycle of abuse.

I tried desperately to cover up what was going on behind my closed doors, partly due to not wanting to accept my reality and partly because I was fearful of the backlash of exposing his bad behaviour, particularly given his violent tendencies.

I had so many fears that kept me awake at night...

Would anyone believe me?

After all, he came across as such a doting husband and proud new father.

At face value he appeared to be looking after his family!

How would I survive financially if I left?

After getting pregnant, I'd been coerced into being heavily dependent on him in every way, the biggest being financially. My confidence had been beaten out of me and the fire in my belly and belief in myself had shattered.

And what would people think of me if I broke up my family?

We get married for better or worse, right?

This is what I'd grown up believing and I wanted so much for my daughter to have a normal family unit.

I fought so hard to give her what she rightly deserved, but it was never meant to be.

It takes two people to make a marriage work and it requires both parents to be emotionally and psychologically stable to create a happy and secure home for any child.

As bad as things were, his excessive drinking was about to make our life so much worse.

Not only did my delightful husband lock me and our 18-month-old daughter out of our family home.

But the stress and anxiety had begun compromising my health.

I soon found myself not only dodging bullets of abuse but also fighting for my life after experiencing a perforated bowel and a rare Cancer diagnosis... all whilst single-handedly trying to keep life as normal as possible for our daughter.

Despite everything I'd gone through, I kept that window of hope open for another four years, thinking he would eventually see sense but I was kidding myself.

What should have made us stronger, actually did the opposite.

In fact, things got a whole lot worse, if that was even possible.

Typical narcissist style, watching me at my lowest point, afraid of what the future looked like for me and our daughter, made him feel more powerful, resulting in me getting even more abuse throughout the best part of my recovery and treatment.

And when I wasn't getting abuse, I was on pins, wondering when he was either going to have yet another one of his drunken, abusive episodes or abandon me and our child again whilst I was at my most vulnerable.

You see, a narcissist preys on vulnerability!

But what he underestimated was the inner strength I knew I still had buried deep within me.

---

***"A crisis doesn't create character... it reveals it"***

---

This was the moment I woke up from the fantasy and the ongoing manipulation I had played along with for far too long.

And that's where my journey began – to build my resilience and breaking free.

So, you see I've been exactly where you are now...

Firstly, I want you to know I hear you; I believe you, and I've got you!

One of my biggest turning points was having a level of acceptance and seeing my marriage for what it was.

A big part of that was understanding my abuser.

Let me tell you, this knowledge doesn't just serve you in breaking away from your abuser, this knowledge is priceless when it comes to divorcing an abuser with narcissistic traits.

Be prepared for delays and more delays when it comes to divorcing them, some of which may even leave you scratching your head in complete disbelief.

But just understand these delay tactics are a means of them keeping a level of control over you and intimidate you from a distance.

This shouldn't come as any surprise given the way they have conducted themselves throughout your relationship, but all these games ramp costs up extortionately, which was a cost I couldn't sustain.

Therefore, I decided to say goodbye to my legal representative and begin training as a McKenzie friend, which has allowed me to navigate my way through the family court system at a fraction of the cost of a solicitor.

I'm not going to tell you it's all plain sailing from there because there are always going to be processes you can't control when engaging with the family court system, but being in control of my own applications and communications meant I was able to make progress much quicker and everything became more streamline.

Now I'm able to support you through the same process so you don't have to sit in the darkness feeling more and more overwhelmed, uncertain and afraid, watching your life spiral further out of control while legal costs just keep stacking up.

Throughout this book, I'm not only going to take you on a journey of self-discovery to pull yourself out from the pits of despair, but I'm also going to walk you through the exact tools I used to build my resilience and enable me to break free safely from the debilitating cycle of abuse I had experienced for years.

I'm also going to show you how to break through your limiting beliefs that not only lead you into an abusive relationship, but also hold you back from doing what you know in your heart you need to do.

So, join me throughout this book so I can support you in taking back control of your future and moving forward feeling stronger and healthier than you did before.

I genuinely look forward to supporting you in... BREAKING FREE... BREAKING THROUGH

AND FLOURISHING to a happier and brighter future for you and your children.

And always remember...

Healing is a journey, not a destination

Kate xx

# QUICK OVERVIEW BEFORE WE GET STARTED

The first thing I would like to do is give you a great big virtual hug for being brave enough to take the first step to healing and breaking the trauma bond that's kept you trapped in this toxic situation.

Before we get started on your journey to self-discovery, I'm just going to give you a bit of an overview of the process I am about to take you on throughout the book.

There are essentially three versions of you that require attention:

### THE FIRST IS YOUR ADULT SELF.

This is all about building resilience, learning to self-sooth and finding "you" again - reconnecting with your values and what's important to you.

An important part of this process is forward planning to ensure a safe exit.

Throughout this whole process, yours and your children's safety has to be the number one priority.

I'm also give you some resilience building exercises to practice with your children. Implementing these and teaching them as early as possible to self-regulate is vital to avoid too much long-term damage from the situation they have been exposed to.

As you will soon discover, the reason you have been drawn into these toxic relationships is as a result of emotional wounds brought about through childhood events, so it's important we, as mothers, break this cycle for our children.

---

### *"HEAL YOURSELF TO HEAL THE NEXT GENERATION."*

---

NEXT IS YOUR YOUNGER SELF, OTHERWISE KNOWN AS YOUR INNER CHILD.

This is the part that's holding onto all the emotional baggage, making you feel de-regulated, overwhelmed and simply not good enough.

It's your wounded younger self that's currently trapped in the trauma bond cycle and afraid to break away in case those old wounds get exposed.

What this part of us doesn't realise is, by protecting you from feeling a wound, it is causing you to experience pain regardless.

It thinks this current emotional distress is less painful than what it is trying to protect you from.

Our job is to establish what the fear centre is trying to protect you from, so we can process that event and move on and make healthier choices.

In this step, we will be connecting very much with how that younger self is feeling, what emotions are coming up and establishing what that parts role is.

Throughout this step, we will be working on soothing and making that younger self feel safe, secure and loved.

We will also make a start on addressing some of the emotional encoding embedded on the fear centre, to switch off that part of our internal alarm system.

THE FINAL STEP TO THE HEALING PROCESS IS UP LEVELLING OUR FUTURE SELF.

This is where I have you connect with your goals and your hopes for the future.

Together, we condition your unconscious mind to see anything is possible, and plan those next steps to bringing these goals into your reality.

This is what's known as post traumatic growth, the process where we take our past pain and turn it into a victory.

Access your book resources on the below link. These will be needed as you work through the content;

https://traumaandanxietybreakthrough.com/book-resources/

---

*"All You Need Is a Little Faith Trust and Pixie Dust."*

---

# TAKING THAT VERY IMPORTANT STEP AS YOUR ADULT SELF

 HAT ARE YOUR REASONS FOR HEALING?

This is going to be your very first journaling exercise. I want you to write down at least 20 reasons for healing and breaking away from your current toxic relationship.

If you can come up with more, fabulous - the more, the better.

This is about giving the unconscious mind valid reasons the current conditions are not in your best interest.

Currently, your brain thinks it is doing a great job at keeping you safe and will look for reasons or attempt to make sense of someone's bad behaviour to avoid feeling another emotional wound, such as abandonment.

- They didn't mean it.
- They are having a bad day.
- They've been drinking (This was a big reason I used for years).

After all, if there is a reason for someone's behaviour, we can fix it, right?

Unfortunately, for that to happen the other person must acknowledge how their behaviour has impacted you or another person. Then be willing to do something about it!

Abusers with narcissistic tendencies don't see the error in their ways.

On occasions, they can tell you what you want to hear, however words without consistent change are just words!

Abusers are experts at faking remorse.

Initially, coming up with 20 reasons is going to be a challenge because it's easy to lose sight of what's important to you after investing so much energy in a man who has shown you little appreciation over the years.

Therefore, to start you off, I'll give you one very good reason - and that is your health and the wellbeing of your children.

You may be able to draw off multiple reasons just from this one subject.

I want you to ask yourself the following questions as honestly as you can...

- How would the deterioration of your health impact your children's lives?
- How would issues with your health or your children's health impact your ability to earn money?
- Do you have anyone to support you with childcare if you were to get unwell?

I know these are things we generally don't like to think about, but these are things we cannot brush under the carpet.

Please learn from my bitter experiences, despite having Crohn's disease, I genuinely thought I was made of steel.

After remaining drug and symptom free for so many years, following a strict approach to diet and lifestyle, I slipped into a false sense of security.

Little did I know what was bubbling away in the background as a result of the ongoing abuse I had experienced since having my daughter.

The physical effects of Anxiety and Trauma really does play havoc on our whole body.

The emotional regulatory ladder pictured below is something you will hear me refer to a lot in many of my trainings and coaching sessions.

EMOTIONAL REGULATORY LADDER

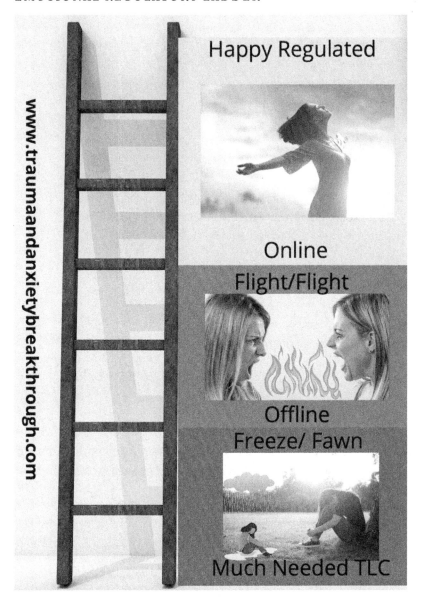

Top of the ladder is where we want to be in our nervous system.

This is where we are regulated, thinking rationally and viewing the world from a place of self, which includes:

- Compassionate
- Calm
- Curious
- Connected
- Confident
- Creative
- Clarity
- Courageous

Many of these qualities we are born with, but have lost them through conditioning from care givers.

These may include curiosity, courageousness, creativity and compassion.

These come naturally to most children in their younger years.

Through conditioning, often, these special qualities are lost.

Calm and regulated is one state that doesn't come naturally.

Even our delivery process is distressing.

It's clinically proven that from 15 weeks in the womb, if our mother is de-regulated, this increased cortisol is passed from mother to baby, causing the babies system to be primed for danger.

The baby therefore arrives into the world hyper vigilant and unable to regulate his/her emotions effectively, and this continues throughout childhood and into adulthood.

Likewise, if your caregivers display little compassion to others, or tiptoe through life afraid to take any chances in life, this is how we will be conditioned to respond within our own surroundings.

This is where our association with love or wealth is formed.

We are a product of our environment.

This means our nervous system defaults to sympathetic as safe, because we are conditioned for survival.

When we react in fight or flight, we are approaching the world judgementally, defensive, angry.

This is where feelings of anxiety start to creep in.

You may even find your anxiety is worse in the mornings. This is because we naturally release cortisol as we wake up to make us alert and reactivate memory and cognitive function to prepare for the day ahead.

This means, if you are already experiencing anxiety due to being in your sympathetic by default, you are likely to experience much higher level of cortisol due to that natural morning release in cortisol.

Our dreams can also have an impact on morning anxiety.

Cortisol is released due to our response to fear.

Fear is triggered by our senses.

We may notice an increase in heart rate, just as you would if you had to run away from danger in a real-life situation. Your brain and body are responding to what it believes is a risk to your safety.

Imagine having to run from danger for days, weeks, or even months with no rest.

What stress do you think that would put on the body?

When our body is flooded with cortisol, this results in inflammation, and inflammation is the result of many chronic health conditions. Inflammation and stress will certainly make the recovery process more challenging when it comes to any health matter.

IBS, IBD and many other auto immune conditions are as a result of inflammatory symptoms.

IBD stands for INFLAMMATORY BOWEL DISEASE and IBS, which is extremely common, is INFLAMMATORY BOWEL SYMPTOMS. Straight away you can see how inflammation plays a primary role in these two conditions.

Auto immune disease and Fibromyalgia also have inflammation and pain as their main symptoms.

Inflammation also encourages cancer cells to grow.

Therefore, gaining control of my psychological state was vital to not only manage my Crohn's but also ensuring I remained free from the big C.

And if Cortisol is causing enough chaos all on its own, when our Sympathetic system is activated, it disables the main nerve in our Parasympathetic system. The Vegus nerve runs from the base of our brain all the way down to our gut, branching off to all the major organs.

Fight or flight is not designed to be a long-term state. Therefore, when the brain needs to preserve energy to either fight or run from danger, it looks to:

- slow down our organ function. This leads to problems in blood pressure, also increasing strain on the heart.
- slow down the immune response.
- reduce the body's ability to regulate inflammation.
- completely shut down the digestive system, leading to raised acidity, damaged gut flora, digestive problems, nutritional deficiencies and inflammation.

Therefore, the steps required to preserve energy are only meant to occur in short bursts, long enough to get us out of danger. Think of a predator chasing it's prey.

Because our human brains struggle to let go of negative emotions and process distressing events, our nervous system always acts as if it is preparing for battle. It cannot differentiate between what's real danger and perceived danger. This puts immense strain on our whole body, leading to the onset of many health problems.

Check out my video in the resource area where I explain the vegus nerve and how it affects organ and immune function in more detail.

Another problem that can occur whilst stuck in this stressed response is that the body can store fat as a way of storing energy. If you have struggled with weight, this could be part of the problem. I will go into this in more detail when we start looking at parts in the younger self.

Additionally, if you're an active gym goer and you're struggling to tone muscle, this again could be as a result of Cortisol flooding the system.

Some of the classic symptoms of fight flight are:

- Clammy hands;
- Raised heart rate;
- An overwhelming fear or dread;
- Responding defensively;
- Aggression.

And finally, as we slip further down that emotional regulatory ladder, we enter freeze and fawn.

These are also part of the sympathetic response but the further down the ladder we get, the more disconnected from the world we become.

Freeze presents with the classic symptoms of depression:

- Getting out of bed is an effort;
- Loss of interest in engaging with friends or family;

- Avoiding crowded places and feeling a sense of panic;
- Feeling more lethargic;
- Maybe you are turning to alcohol or other drugs as a way of numbing out and disconnecting with the overwhelming feeling of emptiness.

These are all classic symptoms of being in freeze.

Fawn is generally where you may find yourself pandering to your abuser and becoming submissive - trying smooth the waters in the hope that you can make everything better. You may even find yourself accepting the blame for something and apologising to your abuser for making them cross.

Another thing you could be experiencing is a nervous cough, as if you frequently need to clear your throat. This is a combination of the vegus nerve tightening up the muscles all around the throat and unspoken anger being held in that area.

There's a great exercise to relieve this in the self-regulation tools

Hopefully you've managed to pull a few things away from that to support you in coming up with your list of reasons to heal but keep adding to that list as you make your way through the book.

---

*"Daily Consistency Is Key to Consistent Results."*

---

RECAP ON TASK 1

1) Make a list of 20 or more reasons why it is important to heal from the ongoing abuse you have been experiencing in your relationship.

2) Journal on these things as much as you possibly can, thinking about what it would feel like if these areas of your

life were to improve or change for the better and journal on how the current situation is impacting your life negatively now.

3) Complete a strengths test using the link in resources. This is useful to do on a monthly basis to keep track of your progress. What I would really love you to do, is complete the form yourself but also ask a close friend or relative who is aware of your current difficulties if they would be happy to complete the same form for you honestly.
The reason for this suggestion is quite often, while we are healing, we can be unfairly judgemental on ourselves, so it is good to get the perspective from two different angles.

4) Make a list of five people who are a toxic influence in your life and how they impact your life negatively. Think about the emotions that come up and the stories you attach to their behaviour (examples of this... I am not good enough, I am not lovable, I am not worthy, I'm to blame).

5) Journal the emotions each of these people have you feeling and what you dislike about their behaviour. Also, think about what would have to change for you to feel better about being around these people. Then ask yourself honestly if this change is possible.

6) Make a list of five positive influences in your life. Again, think about how they make you feel.

7) Journal on these five people and how they make you feel, and focus on how they add value to your life.

8) Think about how you could begin to spend more time with the people who are a positive influence and less time with the people who bring drama to your life.

9) Download your visual in the resources to keep a track and become familiar with your emotional regulatory state.

I have a video lesson as part of the resources to explain how to use this for yourself and your children. Having an awareness of this is important to be able to calm your system down and bring your emotional state back online where you're able to think and act more clearly and rationally, but also reduce the impact stress has on your overall wellbeing. You will be working more with these visuals once you're familiar with the regulatory tools in the next section.

10) Write a bucket list of things you would love to do and pick three that you may be able to start sooner rather than later. This could also be an opportunity to meet or make new friends.

11) Make a list of things you used to love doing before your current/ex relationship and would like to start back up. Again, this could be an opportunity to make new friends and connections.

12) Become aware of your everyday surroundings, taking into consideration your five senses.

**Sight**

Is your home visually comforting? What could you do to make subtle changes to improve how your homely surroundings to make you feel more uplifted?

**Sound**

Do you like to have any music on in the background that makes you feel happy and uplifted? Maybe put together a play list of music that makes you feel good.

**Smell**

Are there any smells that instantly make you feel happy or calm?

Or, likewise, are you wearing a perfume that reminds you of your abusive partner or any other person who is a toxic influence in your life? These are the things we need to be avoiding and replacing with smells that are not activating for our nervous system.

**Taste**

Think about how well you are nourishing your body. Is it supporting your healing process? I'll be covering more on nutrition further in the book.

Maybe you like mints or fruity sweets, these are all fine to suck on if they will stimulate the senses from a happy and regulated perspective but look for the sugar free options as consuming too much sugar, as I will cover in the nutritional section, won't support your healing process.

**Touch**

Think about the soft furnishings in your home how do they make you feel when you touch them? How cosy is your bedding? I know I love soft fleecy things and often snuggle up with a fluffy throw watching a movie with my daughter.

Think about what colours make you feel happy and calm and incorporate these colours into your soft furnishings and wardrobe. Even if it's a scarf, throw or accessory, having colours that you associate with happiness and peace can support the other tools I'm going to cover with you next.

https://traumaandanxietybreakthrough.com/**book-resources/**

# SELF REGULATION TOOLS/ EXERCISES

JOURNALING:

*J*ournaling helps keep your brain in tip-top shape. Not only does it boost memory and comprehension, but it also increases working memory capacity, which may reflect improved cognitive function.

Journaling the negative thoughts is a good brain-dump exercise.

Once you have brain-dumped all the negative thoughts whirling around in your head, immediately replace with something positive. If you are unable to come up with a solution to your specific issue, bring your attention to something that makes you smile.

---

*"The brain cannot focus on positive and negative all at the same time."*

---

But equally, as we can journal out our frustrations, it is also highly beneficial to do the same for anything that's going good in your life.

The more parts of the brain we can activate to the positives in our life, the more it conditions our system in feeling safe.

Here are a few more ideas for journaling prompts to engage in each day:

## GRATITUDE:

Connecting each day with what we are grateful for is a good habit to get into.

It immediately moves our attention away from what's going wrong in our life and back to what is good in our life.

This makes gratitude not only a good journaling exercise, but also a powerful visualisation exercise to use in meditation, hypnosis, and even using my bilateral breakthrough method.

## SMILE AND HUGGING:

Never underestimate the power of a smile and a loving hug with a friend or loved one. It floods the body with all those essential feel-good hormones, filling us with a sense of contentment. Even smiling at someone on the street is incredibly powerful and sends an instant uplifting message to the brain. Just notice the next time someone smiles at you on the street, you will find it difficult not to smile back. And do the same in reverse, smile at a random stranger and notice how many people smile back.

## SELF-LOVE / SELF CARE:

Self-love can come in many forms which is why I have brought these two things together.

Self-love is self-care and promotes the release of our feel-good hormone, putting the brakes on the sympathetic system.

Think about what you can do to pamper yourself and make yourself feel better.

This doesn't always have to involve spending lots of money...

- Run yourself a nice bubble bath with a lovely bath bomb or bubble bar.
- Have some quiet time to do some of the relaxation exercises I'll take you through in your resource area.
- Go for a walk and listen to some uplifting or relaxing music.
- Paint your nails.
- Have a good old girly catch up over a cuppa, either virtually or in person.
- Treat yourself to a massage or a spa day. Daily deal sites are great for these if you're on a budget.
- Book into the hairdressers for a cheeky blow dry.
- Engage in a good daily skin care routine; having a glow to your skin will naturally make you feel better.

There are so many things you can do to give yourself that much needed pick me up, but whatever you chosen form of self-care, ensure you savour every moment to let your system know its ok and safe to feel good.


FAITH:

Faith is a powerful motivator when things are not going good in our lives. Faith allows us to move forward with confidence and avoid worrying about future outcomes. Faith allows us to move forward knowing everything is going to work out. Faith can be found in people, religion or spirituality or even ourselves.

Faith was an important one for me when I was going through my treatment for my Sarcoma.

Fighting the big C is challenging, but throw in a recent bowel operation and dodging bullets of abuse from the man I expected to support me, faith was needed in abundance. I remember experiencing one of my darkest days, terrified what the future looked like for me and my daughter - it was faith and hope which got me through it.

One thing I had was unshakable FAITH in my Orthopaedic Surgeon. I knew I was being taken care of by the best of the best, and both him and his amazing nurses made me feel I wasn't in this alone. Knowing they had my back clinically was a huge weight off my shoulders.

When leaving my abusive marriage, I drew faith from myself.

My faith was in myself.

If I can survive a perforated bowel, a Sarcoma, dodge bullets of abuse all whilst looking after my 3-year-old single handed, well ladies, that makes me Wonder Woman.

Think about who or what you could draw faith from to support you in moving forward with more confidence. Find your anchor of faith and use this as another journaling exercise.

Don't worry too much if you can't quite find anything or anyone to draw faith from because this is where hope will tide you over until faith arrives.


HOPE:

Hope will carry you through the storm.

Try think of a past event, either directly involving yourself or it could be associated with somebody you know.

Where a challenging situation was faced but everything turned out amazingly or better than expected.

Use this as your anchor of hope.

---

*"What if seemingly impossible miracles can happen."*

---

Faith and Hope are very similar, only faith is an unshakable belief that everything is going to work out just fine. Hope re-directs your attention to what is possible.

I used the example for faith when I was going through my Sarcoma recovery and how it helped get me through one of the most difficult times of my life.

The same applied to HOPE.

My anchor of hope through that time was my mum.

My mum, although she has sadly passed away, defied the odds with various cancers for years. Having witnessed seemingly impossible miracles with my own eyes, it gave me the hope I needed to believe my outcome could be favourable too.

I then used that same approach when finally going no contact and filing for divorce, like you are now.

I was scared and uncertain of what the future looked like, so I the drew courage I needed from my mentor, Caroline, and took that leap of faith.

She was my beacon of hope.

Whenever I lost my way, I would draw my focus back to how her life was when she left her Narcissist and how her life now is so much better.

And I want you to do the same. Draw your hope from me and other women who have come through the storm stronger, and choose to believe that you can too.

Write every day as part of your journaling exercises:

"**WHAT IF** seemingly impossible miracles can come into my life and change everything for the better"

Then follow on with your anchor of hope. The importance is repeatedly feeding this into the unconscious mind until you can gain faith in your outcome.

The importance is in the **WHAT IF**.

Currently, your fear centre and your unconscious mind may not believe life can be as magical as you envisage. But it can. We just need to convince our unconscious mind that positive change is possible.


AFFIRMATIONS:

Which brings me onto getting the most out of your affirmations.

You may have done affirmations a million times, yet they don't make the slightest bit of difference.

I have bought so many mindset courses, I have lost count. One of the things I learnt from one my wonderful mentors was affirmations only work if the amygdala (our fear centre) is on-board with the suggestion.

**For example:**

I AM SUCCESSFUL, I AM ENOUGH, I AM WORTHY, I AM HAPPY.

I could have said these things until I was blue in the face. I even had I AM ENOUGH written on my mirrors. No matter how many times I made these bold statements, my amygdala was sitting silently, rolling its eyes and thinking I was chatting utter nonsense.

This is because my words did not match my reality. But not only that, I had an army of protector parts showing up, preventing me from feeling an emotional wound, which also highlighted my self-belief wound of not being good enough.

When I refer to protector part, I am referring to things like:

- Procrastination.
- People pleasing.
- Stage fright.
- Aggression.

I'll talk about these more later in the book, but these parts will make any firm statements you make completely ineffective or not long lasting.

The only way to resolve this issue long-term, is to eliminate the event specific biological markers embedded on the fear centre responsible for these parts showing up to protect you. This is where the psycho sensory methods come into their own. Again, I will be covering this with you when we get to younger self.

In the meantime, we can be getting the unconscious mind on-board with the possibility of change. By simply tweaking your affirmation process slightly with WHAT IF, or I DESERVE, starts to prime the unconscious mind to a better outcome.

WHAT IF I could be successful, how would that improve the opportunities available to me?

WHAT IF I have always been worthy of success, happiness, and freedom?

I DESERVE to achieve success because that would improve not just my life, but that of those I love and cherish.

Now, although these are a lot of firm statements, you can take those statements and tweak accordingly if you feel any resistance.

Once you start to believe that within your system, without any resistance to the suggestion, move onto: I CAN, I WILL, I DESERVE.

These are firmer statements, without telling the unconscious mind lies.

And only once you move closer to achieving your goal, move to I AM.

A good app I like to use is the I AM app which you can download from iTunes for a small annual fee.

What I love about this app is you can set up alerts to come up however many times a day you like, and you can pick the topic you want them to be on. It's a great reminder to keep you in a state of positivity rather than negative.

HAPPY FEELINGS AND MEMORIES:

Make a list of 10 happy memories to visualise and connect with. Do this as if you are recreating these events in your mind.

Next, make a list of the happy emotions that you experienced at the time and the happy emotions you experience whilst recreating that same event through your visualisation process. These are all good things to turn to while utilising the meditation exercises, I show you and the psycho sensory methods also.

YOUR BEST QUALITIES:

Make a list of 20 or more of your best qualities. Journal these out and read them each day to remind yourself just how amazing you are.

COLD WATER:

Either splashing your face with ice cold water OR having a cold shower will send an electric signal to the brain to release dopamine and condition the nervous system that it is safe, despite the experience being unpleasant.

Dopamine is a neurotransmitter that is released when we feel good and feel stressed and is what promotes addiction. Alcohol or other stimulants such as sugar or even dangerous activities provide us with a rush of dopamine. We experience the same rush of dopamine when we enter a new relationship and experience the initial feeling of attraction. This explains why, for some people, falling in love is so addictive and could lead to multiple affairs or jumping from one relationship to another.

The trick is to provide the brain with its daily doses of dopamine in a way that is not toxic to either ourselves or other people.

The use of cold water is one way you can do that.

Engaging in this regularly also helps to condition the nervous system to not react irrationally to every unpleasant situation.

And a bonus to this cold-water exercise is it does wonders for your skin and hair as it improves blood circulation.

**TIP**: Try short 1 min blasts of very cold water on your face while in the shower, paying close attention to your breath. Initially, the cold water will take your breath away but consciously regulate your breath to support that feeling of safety.

After the 1 min blast, turn it straight back to hot and immerse your body in the warmth to enhance that feeling of safety within your nervous system.

I also find benefit in holding my chest and abdomen under the cold shower too. I haven't specifically come across any evidence of this providing benefit, but we know there are neurons in the heart and the gut, which is why we feel so many emotions around these areas. And I certainly find benefit in this cold-water approach.

It is also beneficial to drink ice cold water as this can stimulate the vegus nerve when we swallow, instructing the body to relax.

**Important: If you have epilepsy or psychosis, please seek consent from your health care provider before engaging in cold water therapy.**

## HYPNOSIS:

Hypnosis allows us to go deep into the unconscious mind, and because it slows the brain frequency down to Theta, it offers amazing healing benefits.

Some benefits of hypnosis are:

- Supports the reframing of our negative belief system.
- Supports overcoming phobias.
- Supports overcoming addictions.
- Promotes better sleep.
- Supports pain management.

## MEDITATION:

Meditation is essentially the induction process of hypnosis that gently encourages the mind and body to relax so we can more easily access the unconscious mind.

Meditation can vary greatly from light meditated to a much deeper meditative state, but our aim is to slow the mind down so we can better process our thoughts and emotions, allowing us to hit the brakes on the fight/flight response and improve vegal tone.

Meditation can last anything from 5 minutes to 30 minutes and is a good exercise to implement into your daily routine as a means of keeping you regulated.

Meditation is a great way to utilise your visualisation exercises and gratitude.

Meditation doesn't always have to be sitting quietly and floating up into the clouds, it can be a simple as visualising and using imagination to tell a story. This makes this kind of meditation beneficial to use with children of all ages.

Children's imaginations are so much more creative and visual than adults so you will be able to take them on a magical adventure into their imagination very easily.

There are many other versions of meditation that you can tap into. Some of the methods I use are techniques that implement conscious breathing, VOO or OMMM Sounds.

I demonstrate some of these in the resource library.

DIAPHRAGMATIC AND RESONANT FREQUENCY BREATHING:

Breath work is a good thing to practice every day. When we are in fight/flight our breathing naturally becomes more erratic and we take shorter breaths. By becoming consciously aware of our breathing, slowing it down and ensuring we are breathing from the belly, this gives our nervous system a sense of safety.

If we were really in danger, we wouldn't be able to control our breath.

There's a demonstration of this in your resource area.

MINDFULNESS:

Mindfulness can be integrated into so many things in our day-to-day life and is good to practice with children to get them out of the emotional part of their brain.

Here are a couple of ideas you can easily implement:

Activating the 5 senses... 5 things you can see, 4 things you can touch, 3 things you can hear, 2 things you can smell, and 1 thing you can taste. (For taste I like to encourage people to start keeping sugar free mints or boiled sweets in their bag or pocket so they can easily stimulate this sense.)

- In the shower is a great place to be mindful. Close your eyes and notice the water on your face, notice the relaxing feeling as you massage the shampoo into your scalp.
- Massaging cream into your skin. Really be intentional when applying creams.

Eating food. This is a thing so many people rush, and this not only impacts the digestive process, but we don't enjoy food as much as we could. On your next meal, eat slowly and put your knife and folk down between each mouth full, notice the different tastes and textures of the food.

- Having time away from social media or TV to play a game with the kids and just be fully present.
- Go on a mindful walk with the kids or on your own.

Focus your awareness on surroundings activating the 5 senses.

- Art therapy is a popular mindfulness exercise.

This is something that is incredibly powerful with children to help them express how they are feeling but also bring them make to present moment.

The use of colour in art also can influence how we feel, so be aware of what colours are associated with different emotions when partaking in art therapy.

Art therapy can also include purchased art to hang in your home.

There are so many ways to be mindful; mindfulness is just being present and in the moment, not thinking ten steps ahead or trying to do five things at once, which I know us mums are guilty of doing a lot.

## POWER OF SHIFTING YOUR STATE:

We can shift our state in an instant just by changing our posture, sitting up straight, pulling your shoulders and lifting your head up. You will find when you do this it is difficult to look or feel miserable. You instantly want to smile.

The other thing you can do is get up and move your body, whether that's dancing or walking, the bilateral movement not only stimulates the feel-good hormones, but it also activates the two sides of our brain. This why exercise is so good for our mental state of mind.

I talk more about bilateral stimulation below.

One thing to bear in mind if you are experiencing anxiety on a regular basis, engaging in too much high impact cardio, will significantly raise the heart rate. This reminds the brain you are in a life-threatening situation, which will, in turn, keep you in survival state. The reason for this is, when we are in danger our instinct is to run, which increases our heart rate, and adrenaline pumps round the body. Therefore, if we are frequently in our sympathetic system, running could alert our internal alarm system that danger is still present.

Whilst healing from any trauma responses, my advice would be engaging in lighter exercise/ movement such as walking, resistance training, Pilates, yoga or swimming, which are all good options and amazing for shifting your state from negative to positive whilst keeping the nervous system regulated.

We can also shift our state by dancing, singing or listening to happy uplifting music. Think about what your soul needs and choose your playlist accordingly. Maybe you need to feel inspired and motivated for your business or career, or maybe you need to feel that loving and romantic feeling. Whatever your soul is craving, choose the music that will feed your soul.

Think about your surroundings in the home. Does a certain smell make you feel relaxed and calm? Do you find certain textures comforting?

Bring in colours you associate with happiness, peace and fulfilment. Really activate and draw as many of the senses towards the positive in the home or office.

The same principles can apply to accessories and clothing.


POWER OF FORGIVENESS:

I know this may at first be a tough thing to do and you're probably thinking why you should forgive your abuser's bad behaviour.

It isn't about forgiving their behaviour. It is about letting go of the energy behind the emotion that is eating you up and keeping you in a state of unease.

***ANGER AND RESENTMENT IS LIKE DRINKING POISON AND EXPECTING THE OTHER PERSON TO DIE!***

Sadly, the other person doesn't feel any emotion knowing you are angry with them. Your abuser is not capable of feeling true emotions for anyone, so let it go, for your own sake.

A good exercise for this is:

Visualise the person behind your closed eyes and repeat the phrase:

"I'm sorry, please forgive me, thank you, I love you."

Repeat this three times, then imagine a cord between you and that person and cut the cord with a virtual pair of golden scissors. As you witness the cord start to drift away repeat the phrase again.

This is a good exercise to do on the full moon and new moon.

TAPPING:

There are a couple of ways to incorporate tapping. There's tapping on the meridian points around the face, collar bone, hand and wrist.

This is known as EFT.

But a form of tapping I use sometimes, along with positive visualisation exercises, is resource tapping, which is a method used in EMDR.

By gently tapping in a bilateral motion whilst dropping into a happy feeling, it taps in the feeling of safety and calm into the nervous system.

I demo this for you in the resource area.

BILATERAL STIMULATION:

Bilateral movement or bilateral stimulation activates the left and right parts of the brain. By activating the two hemispheres of the brain, we enhance the processing and filing of memories and data.

Ways we can utilise bilateral stimulation are:

- Bilateral music which is sound that moves from the left to right ear when listened to through headphones.
- Walking is a form of bilateral movement, although usually best incorporating this with bilateral music at the same time to benefit fully.
- Tapping your legs left to right which is a form of resource tapping.

## BILATERAL BREAKTHROUGH METHOD:

This method, which I developed, incorporates the use of delta waves through specific touch, palm stimulation and bilateral movement. This effectively enables us to access the fear centre in the brain which is where all these unwanted emotions are embedded.

To properly address the deeply embedded activation wounds we first must slow our brain frequency down to delta, which in turn, makes the brain more pliable, enabling us to dislodge the event specific biological markers responsible for the ongoing activation we experience from trauma.

This technique can be used very easily as a self-regulation tool, which I will demonstrate for you in the resource area, OR it can be used when we start working on those activation wounds.

## EYELINE ACTIVATION POINTS:

You may not have consciously noticed, but when we're thinking, or searching our memory banks for words while engaged in conversation or trying to remember past information, we usually move our line of vision or gaze intently to one point as if searching for the answers.

For most people this represents looking into the past for answers.

This point in our line of vision can often activate our system, so it is good to become aware of where this activation point is and where your non-activation point is also. This awareness will prevent you from keeping your focus on a point that is triggering to the system. This is certainly something to be aware of if you have any court hearings or interviews.

I demonstrate this in the resource area, so I certainly encourage you to check this out as it will support you when engaging in any mindfulness exercises, and generally day-to-day, to support keeping your system regulated.

## SLEEP AND ACTIVATING YAWNING:

Good quality Sleep is incredibly important, not just for the healing and rejuvenation of the whole body but also for processing and storing memories and emotions. It is specifically the two later stages of sleep that support these roles.

Non-REM - stage 3, and REM, which means we have to go through Non-stages 1 and 2 before healing and processing can take place.

Therefore, disturbed sleep is so impactful on our overall health and wellbeing.

Things that can support a better night sleep:

- Coming away from electrical devices an hour before bed and try unwinding with some theta music, meditation or breath work. This will really help to slow your brain frequency down to one that will support restful sleep.
- Avoid any cardio exercising in the evening, this will promote the release of Cortisol and adrenalin, causing the heart rate to go up, which won't support a good restful sleep or support the repair and regeneration of muscle.
- Get into a good sleep routine by waking up and going to

sleep and the same time every day. This helps the body clock optimise for a full night's sleep.

- If you do wake up in the night to go to the bathroom, avoid using the main lights. Try keeping the lighting as dimmed as you can so it is easier to get back to sleep.
- Try drifting off to Theta or Delta music or Hypnosis.
- Avoid heavy meals in the evening, try to plan your meals so you are having any heavy or hard to digest meals at lunch time or no later than early evening, otherwise the digestion process will hinder your sleep process.
- Avoid alcohol, nicotine and caffeine as these can all hinder the sleep cycle.

Yawning is also the brains way of preparing the body to relax deeply for sleep as it tones and stimulates the Vegus nerve. There is a useful technique you can use to stimulate yawning and support the parasympathetic system at any time of the day. I demonstrate this in the resource area.

The importance of toning the Vegus nerve for nervous system regulation:

You will have noticed I have referred to the Vegus nerve quite a few times whilst taking you through the above self-regulatory tools, and this is because it is a key part of keeping the body operating optimally. By actively engaging in the positive loop systems, switching negative thoughts to positive, that puts the breaks on our sympathetic system and the brain instructs all the organs to relax. It does this via the Vegus nerve. By regularly toning the Vegus Nerve and accessing that positive loop system, we not only improve organ function, but we also improve heart rate variability, we increase oxygen exchange, lower blood pressure and, very importantly, we regulate our body's inflammatory response, improving immune response and digestion.

The other thing people can often notice when they are holding onto anger, is experiencing an annoying, nervous cough. It feels like you are forever needing to clear your throat.

Just as the vegus nerve branches off to our various organs, impacting how well they are operating, we also have a branch off to the throat and it can cause this area to tighten up, which is why voo or resonant frequency breathing is so good for helping relax this area.

You can see just how important these regulatory tools are for our overall well-being.

https://traumaandanxietybreakthrough.com/book-resources/

---

*"The Flower That Blooms Despite Adversity, Is The Rarest & Most Beautiful Flower Of All."*

---

# SAFETY EXIT PLAN

*Y*our exit plan is an important process to consider when leaving any abusive relationship.

Quite often when an abusive partner realises you are planning on leaving, the abuse can ramp up. Not only does the emotional abuse increase, but this is also the time physical safety is more at risk.

An exit plan is designed to help you consider all your options and implement steps to limit the risk to yourself or children.

A narcissist who has a history of coercive and controlling behaviour, once discarded is a higher risk of engaging in seriously assaulting, even resorting to murder.

You may have heard or read about past cases where women have sadly lost their lives at the hands of their abuser once they made a stand against them.

I don't say this in any way to frighten you; it is simply to highlight the importance of exiting in the safest possible way for you and your children.

Become aware of low-risk areas in the home where there are no implements that could be used as weapons, and if possible has more than one exit route. If an argument or heated discussion occurs, try move the conversation to this part of the house to avoid any unfortunate mishaps.

Always keep your phone on you - having it discretely in a pocket is preferred so that you can access it easily if you need to call 999 for emergency assistance. Additionally, if you can safely do so you can use your phone to record any event which could later be used as evidence with the police or courts.

Keep your handbag, keys and purse with money or cards in an easily accessible place in case you need to grab them in a hurry.

Talking to children about what to do in an emergency is a vital life skill regardless of there being domestic abuse in the house. Teaching them to call 999 or shout for help if anyone is seriously hurt or unconscious, or in case of a fire is vital for your current situation.

Unless your children have been directly exposed to the domestic abuse, it is always best to avoid alerting them to the situation until the time is right.

One thing we must be mindful of is being accused of badmouthing the other parent to the children to isolate them, this can work against you when it comes to court and child arrangements, but I'll cover more on this in the divorce section.

Obviously if the children are aware of the situation, then I don't believe in diluting the seriousness of the situation or lying to them in any way because this can also result in trust issues occurring and one thing the children need in a situation like this is certainty that they have one safe person in their life that they can trust. It's very much a case of weighing up and evaluating the conditions your children are exposed to and how much awareness they currently have.

If your children are aware of the situation, encourage them to call for help if things were to escalate, but not to try intervening or to get involved, is always a good idea. Their safety is always paramount, but ensure, dependant on their age, they remember as many of the vital information needed for the emergency services, such as their full name, mummy and daddy's first names, address, and phone number - although this usually shows up on emergency switch board when calling 999.

If you have a neighbour you can trust, let them know about the situation and ask them to call the emergency services if they are concerned at all.

Store in your phone emergency numbers under female friend's names or put these in your notes section such as, domestic abuse help line, doctors, your local police station, children's school, solicitors or McKenzie friend – although as a rule, I wouldn't be encouraging many people to start divorce proceedings until you are safely away.

However not everyone's situation is as extreme as some people's. This is a decision you must weigh up carefully. From my own personal experience, the moment I filed for divorce, my husband become increasingly more vindictive.

Pack an emergency bag for yourself and the children and hide it somewhere safe. If you can't leave it with a friend neighbour, then have this somewhere your abuser won't find it and you can grab easily in a hurry. Ideally, this needs to be out of the family home.

When I think back to when my abuser locked me and our then 18-month-old out, we had nothing other than a small amount of credit on a credit card, which I only had by chance. I had no nappies, no change of clothes, so before checking into a hotel for the night I had to buy everything I needed so I could at least attend to my daughter's immediate needs.

When packing an emergency bag, think about worst case scenario because you may not be able to gain access to the family home immediately.

## Things to consider:

Money/ cards.
Extra set of house or car keys.
A couple of sets fresh clothes for you and the children.
Passports.
Birth certificates.
Marriage certificates.
Any other legal documents you may need for the house or
insurances etc.
Bank details.
Medication.

Any documents related to children.

Discuss with a trusted friend or family member your intention of
breaking away from your abuser. It is important to know where you
are going to be able to stay with your children until you get back on
your feet.

If it's not possible to go to a friend or family member, maybe have an
idea of a couple of hotels you could affordably book into for the
night until you can contact the relevant authorities and women's
refuges.

Now that you have all this vital information and strategies in place,
it's time to talk about what you do once you make that important
brave step.

One of the most dangerous times, as I've mentioned before, is when
you leave your abuser. Statistics show that 75% of women are at risk
of being killed at the hands of their abuser and no more so than an
abuser with narcissistic tendencies. The moment you open their
abandonment wounds, you're no longer the women they moulded
and controlled throughout the relationship; you become enemy
number one and they will punish you for this in whatever way they

feel warrants the pain you are making them re-experience from their childhood.

Therefore, the very first thing I would encourage you to do after you have a safe roof over yours and your children's head is calling the police and at the very least, get a statement on record about the abuse. If the evidence you can provide the police is strong enough, they could bring them in for questioning and passed over to CPS (Child Protection Service) for further investigation.

This will then provide you with the protection of bail throughout the investigation.

Failing an official investigation, apply to court for an emergency non-molestation order and an occupational order if your family home is owned.

Non-molestation order is an order made by the court which restricts your abuser from directly contacting you or coming within a certain distance of you.

An Occupational order is an order made by a judge around the residence of the family home. The aim in applying for an occupational order in the case of a domestic abuse case is for the judge to order you husband to move out of the family home so you and the children can reside there. The order will usually instruct your partner to not turn up at the family home unless otherwise agreed.

Although I would encourage you to delay initiating divorce proceedings until you are safely away from your abusive partner, I would suggest, if you can, to discreetly complete the printed version of these forms prior to leaving, and have these safely ready to send off to the court the moment you break away, as time is certainly of the essence if the police don't take criminal proceedings.

Another thing you may need to look at if the family home is solely in your partner's name, is applying a residency order on the land registry. This will prevent the other party from selling or borrowing against the property without your say so. This will strengthen your position if you apply to court for an occupational order.

Just a quick note on divorce: I know the cost implications around this can be something that can stop people from making that break and I know that, on top of everything else, it can be overwhelming, but I promise you, you can do this without a solicitor, and even if you decide to invest in representation for court, you can save an absolute fortune by doing all the applications yourself.

I am going to take you step by step through the family court process.

## POST SEPARATION AND MAINTAINING SAFETY AROUND CHILD ARRANGEMENTS.

This is where it gets a bit tricky, and you must weigh up the risk to your safety.

The first thing to consider is the age of the children and if they are expressing any wishes to see the other parent.

Whether the children wish to see the other parent or not, I would encourage you to apply for an emergency child arrangements order and complete a section A on this form highlighting the domestic abuse.

Depending on how quickly the court respond, if the children are asking to speak or see the other parent, I would potentially arrange telephone communication which takes place with an external family member or friend present, in case any manipulation or intimidating conversations were to arise whilst they are on the phone to the children.

If, on the other hand, the children are expressing strong wishes not to see the other parent due to their own fear being around them, then as their resident parent you have the right to do what you feel is in their best interest and keeps you all safe and well.

I know some McKenzie friends and solicitors would say wait and see if the other parent applies to court for access, but there are two reasons I decided to initiate this process myself:

The first reason was feeling in control of my own emotions.

For too many years he had dictated and controlled me and sitting, waiting and wondering if or when he was going to apply was leaving me in emotional limbo, which could have potentially gone on for years.

The other reason was by taking the bull by the horns I was able to put the true facts across to CAFCAS from the start. As I was the applicant, it meant it was for my husband to disprove my concerns. Whereas if he had applied, being an abusive narcissist who was in complete denial as to the damage he had caused to myself and our daughter, he was never going to tell the complete truth. There were some things he knew he had to be upfront about because there was no way of talking his way out of these things, but he certainly would have diluted a lot of the facts. That way, being the defendant, it would have been for me to disprove his allegations.

If they really want access to their children, one way or another they will apply and fight to see their children, so you may as well be in the driving seat from the start.

## OTHER THINGS TO CONSIDER

### 1. NO CONTACT IS VITAL AT THIS STAGE OF YOUR RECOVERY!

Change your main day-to-day number and if the children have telephone contact with the other parent, have a dedicated email and cheap phone just for that contact at the arranged time, and have that phone switched off otherwise.

I honestly cannot tell you how much of a difference this makes.

It is hard at first because your system will want to draw you to what's familiar, but, as hard as it feels, please stick it out. If you get the urge to contact them, distract yourself with a meditation or one of the tools I am going to be walking you through. Call a friend or family member instead if you need to get it out of your system.

If you must engage on calls with the children or handovers when child arrangements are firmed up through the courts, it is important to continue to GREY ROCK them.

Show no emotions, appear boring and uninteresting.

2. The other things I want you to consider, once you have arranged accommodation for you and the children, get yourself a security camera.

I know it may seem extreme, but my husband turned up after walking 3 hours, drunk, in the early hours of the morning, which led to his arrest for breaching bail.

3. Contact domestic abuse services for your area if you haven't done so already.

Even if you have support, your local domestic abuse services can assess your risk and potentially have tags put on your address and provide panic buttons. They may also be able to arrange play therapy for the children and coordinate with child services.

4. Let your children's school know immediately of the situation.

Advise them of any court applications and any safeguarding matters they need to consider if the father were to turn up. They know to contact you straight away and update any emergency contact information if necessary.

5. If your ex-partner turns up at the address you and the children live at, call 999 immediately and never arrange for any collections to take place at your address - these must only ever happen in a public place or by another person like a grandparent or other relative who you can trust.

6. Make a list of friends and family that could support you in an emergency if you need it.

---

*"The Journey to Safety & Freedom Begins with A Single Step."*

---

# THE IMPACT DOMESTIC ABUSE
# HAS ON THE CHILDREN

*E*ven if children are not directly in the line of fire, never underestimate the psychological impact witnessing heated or aggressive arguments, ongoing manipulation, addiction and physical abuse in the home has on a child's mental wellbeing. Even when the abuse is only directed towards you, it is believed experiences like this for a child has the same effect on the brain as combat does in soldiers.

Most psychological issues we experience as adults, stem back to being exposed to toxic or emotionally distressing situations as children, particularly during the first seven years, as the brain is developing.

Children who experience ongoing traumatic experiences while their brain is developing have a much higher risk of issues with addictions later in life and suffering ongoing problems with their own mental health, whether that be in the form of Cluster B personality disorder like Narcissism or ending up co-dependent, attracting toxic relationships into their own lives.

Even if the children don't appear afraid of the other parent, this is not a reason to stay. Children can appear to be coping but potentially be at the bottom of their emotional regulatory ladder in freeze or fawn. Fawn would be where they seem to be pandering to the other parent, always seeking to please.

You may also have noticed your child starting to mirror the perpetrators behaviours.

This is a survival technique the brain engages in to keep them safe. This is a common survival tactic for children who are exposed to such situations. This is when the risk increases for them becoming narcissists themselves as they get older.

I'll cover some of the other survival traits to look out for when we get into Inner Child, but it's common for children to blame themselves for the toxic situation, as though the heated arguments and aggression they witness are their fault.

When a child is exposed to ongoing traumatic and distressing situations whilst their brain is developing, it can affect how well the brain produces Serotonin naturally. Additionally, long-term exposure to emotionally distressing situations while the brain is developing creates an increased sensitivity to Dopamine, which can lead to the development of several addictions occurring. Substances and Alcohol being the highest risk due to the concentration of dopamine that is produced compared to shopping, food, gambling and even sex.

It's clinically proven that if a mother is stressed during her pregnancy, from 15 weeks, the cortisol that is being passed down via the umbilical cord, is priming the baby's system to become sensitive to his/her surroundings. This means even before baby is born and experiences life, their system is primed to think the world is dangerous and the fear centre in the brain enlarges accordingly. Bearing in mind that we all are born in fight, flight or freeze, due to the delivery process being stressful, this is why to be calm and regulated, we must be taught how to be this way by our caregivers. However, for a child born with an already enlarged fear centre, the delivery process is much more challenging, so it isn't unusual for these babies to cry a lot or become distressed if they are put down for even a moment. This is due to their system not feeling in any way safe and the only way to feel safe is to have that closeness, usually with their mummy.

This is something I can relate to personally with my daughter.

From the moment I moved away from her she would start to cry, and still, to this day, she needs to know where I am, even in the house.

Even if children appear to have no emotional issues, don't ever underestimate the damage that may be hiding under the surface. It could be that their system is stuck in freeze or fawn, causing them to retreat and quietly play with toys or games.

If they are in fawn, they can appear to be an over pleaser. This could be their system becoming submissive to remain safe.

Studies have shown that children who have grown up or been exposed to domestic abuse or substance misuse in the home are more likely to:

- Use violence at school or in the community in response to perceived threats. Even something as simple as a child not sharing a toy or allowing them to play will be enough to trigger this type of response.
- Be bullied or behave in a bulling way towards other children.
- Display poor concentration and make poor academic progress.
- Show delayed physical development such as speech and walking.
- Be afraid to invite friends to their home in fear of shame of what they may witness.
- Attempt or talk about suicide.
- Engage in alcohol or drug misuse.
- Commit crimes, even sexual assault.

- Become abusers in their own relationships, as I've covered previously.

**When living with domestic abuse children learn:**

- That violence is a way to resolve conflict
- Keeping secrets or telling lies is a normal way to respond when we do something wrong.
- To mistrust those close to them.
- Children often believe they are responsible or to blame for the abuse they witness in the home.

You may be able to relate to a number of these.

I know with my own daughter, after fighting for so long, thinking she was on the autistic spectrum, since doing my training so many of her traits and behaviours are starting to link back to what she has experienced from birth. In fact, certainly, it wasn't until we went no contact with her dad did she start to openly share her fears and insecurities regarding her Daddy. Prior to no contact, she kept it very much to herself.

If you have got a child on the autistic spectrum, try to put the label to one side and consider what is causing them emotional distress to act or behave in the way that they are?

These behaviours are the brain's way of preventing your child from feeling something deeper.

TASKS TO DO WITH YOUR CHILDREN

Start to become aware of where your children are on the emotional regulatory ladder.

I've added two printable versions of these for you to use with your children. My suggestion is getting them printed and laminated and start using these daily.

Ask your child, based on the images, how do they feel?

Younger children tend to struggle to articulate how they are feeling so the visuals are very helpful for you to get to know their nervous system better.

Once they have shown you where they are on the ladder, see if they will openly discuss what's caused them to feel that way. Talk to them about this, offering any reassuring words of comfort to make their system feel safe.

Even if they are at the top of the ladder, if they are willing to share, it is good to identify what sort of things cause them to dip to the different stages of the emotional regulatory ladder.

If they are in a state of distress and you are struggling to get them to express themselves, you will already have an idea as to what may have upset their system and the thoughts and feelings they may be experiencing at that moment, but more importantly, you will already be aware of the things that make them feel safe, so once the situation has defused a little you can start to introduce tools to bring them back up the ladder to safety.

(Check out the Video in resources.)

Make a list with your child of 25 positive statements that describe them, highlighting the things they are good at and all their wonderful qualities.

Make a list of the behaviours that need improving and talk to your child about how they make you and others feel.

Use the emotional regulatory ladder so they can visually see the impact their actions have on other people's feelings.

Always follow up with positive reinforcement.

**Example I use with my little girl:**

When you hurt mummy, it makes me feel sad and it makes me feel broken hearted (and I point to where I am on the ladder).

BUT, I know you are such a kind girl, and you don't want to make mummy sad.

Do you think next time you're feeling angry you could talk to mummy about it first?

Children generally do not want to hurt the feelings of people they love or care about. Their response is driven out of frustration with an emotion that's been triggered. Teaching them to become more aware of their feelings and the possible cause means they are more likely to self-regulate as they get older, and avoid using destructive influences as a way of switching off or self-soothing.

Everything I am covering for you as the adult self and younger self all applies to your children, and by following the tools I am teaching you; you can minimise the risk of psychological problems in the future.

- Make a happy memory box or album with your little one.

This is going to be a tool you can use to bring them back up the ladder to safety. I will be demonstrating and discussing this in a video training in the resource area.

Additional regulation tools you can use with your little ones include mindfulness exercises, using the 5 senses, Singing, Dancing and visualisation, using their imagination through story.

I will cover this in the video training also.

https://traumaandanxietybreakthrough.com/**book-resources**/

---

*"There's Nothing More Powerful Than a Mother's Love &*
*Nothing More Motivating Than Your Child's Happiness."*

---

# DIVORCE ROAD MAP

*F*irst things first, I am in no way telling you not to get a solicitor if that's what you feel more comfortable with, BUT, you absolutely do not need a solicitor to get divorced. In fact, even by instructing a solicitor, you will still end up filling out and completing most of the documentation and they will look over before submitting to the courts.

When I had a solicitor, I constantly felt in the dark. I felt so un-in-control of any of the process, it not only led to an increase in anxiety and uncertainty, but also resulted in me repeatedly emailing or calling for updates, which hiked costs up at an unsustainable rate. Three and half months later and £5000 out of pocket, I was no further forward in the process.

After a good friend recommended McKenzie friend, I decided to explore this option further and decided to complete the training course so I could, at the very least, start to get my head around the family court system and gain clarity on the journey ahead.

After chatting with some experienced McKenzie friends whilst making my way through the training, I quickly started to realise investing in a solicitor, certainly at the administration and filing point, was money down the drain.

Even when it comes to sitting in front of a judge, not even the best and most experienced solicitor or barristers can influence or change the family court process. The process is very structured, and if a judge needs to step in throughout the process, he will make any decision based on the facts that are presented to him/her and always within the best interest of the child.

I don't want you to sit reading this through rose tinted spectacles, thinking if you present the facts then surely it will go in your favour. Sadly, there have been cases where judges haven't acted in the best interest of the children.

But the important thing to take from this is, regardless of if you are being represented by a solicitor or representing yourself, the judge's decision is what it is. I have even heard of occasions where the judge has ignored the recommendations of CAFCAS s, who they appoint to investigate child arrangements and safeguarding matters and advise the courts accordingly based on their findings.

Based on these facts alone, why come out the other end of this process heavily in debt, when with a little guidance and support you can successfully represent yourself for a fraction of the cost?

Therefore, I felt it was important to provide you with a divorce and family court road map so I could set you off in the right path and more importantly, off to a productive start.

If you get to the point of needing to attend court and sit before a judge, and don't feel confident in doing so, then you could assign a solicitor or direct access barrister to represent you at that stage.


FIRST SOME HOUSE RULES:

Avoid mudslinging or name calling. The courts only deal with the facts.

Unless you can back an allegation up with evidence, it will be seen as mudslinging or alienation, which will reflect badly on your case.

Keep all allegations relevant. Some examples of this would be:

- pointing out the other parties past shortfalls and using them against them now to paint them in a worse light. Perhaps he/she got arrested for shop lifting as a teenager. Using this past event to suggest this makes them an unfit parent is a fruitless exercise. Although this behaviour isn't good, it is irrelevant in how good or bad a parent they are to your children.
- "He/she goes out drinking all the time" this would only be relevant if their lifestyle choices impact the children and their safety directly. Are they being around the children under the influence? Is their dependency so severe that it has led to professional intervention? Does it sever enough to warrant professional intervention?
- He/she has been unfaithful. This is relevant as grounds for divorce certainly, but when it comes to child arrangements this wouldn't be relevant unless it effected their parental responsibilities directly
- As certain as you may be that they are a Narcissist, avoid the urge to throw labels around unless there is an official medical diagnosis. The fact we know a narcissist will rarely seek a diagnosis because their behaviours serve a purpose for them, the only thing the judge and the courts are interested in is if their behaviour is criminal or potentially endangering yours or your children's safety and well-being.

This goes back to remaining very factual.

If you can prove unreasonable and abusive behaviour, certainly use everything you can to strengthen your case. Therefore, I want to stress the importance of gaining or keeping as much evidence as you can to back up any claims you make to the courts as well as the police. The police may not proceed with charges, as the requirements for a criminal court are much stricter than in the family courts, but in family courts, you only must put into question their intentions and the courts should, in theory, take all evidence into consideration, particularly were there are safeguarding concerns for minors.

- When in court hearings, only answer what is asked.

Avoid trying to justify or explain the background to your answer.

And that's all you need to remember for court rules. Remain factual and relevant and you cannot go wrong.

## FILING FOR DIVORCE:

Filing for divorce is how you obtain your court ref number.

This will be needed to proceed with any financial or child arrangements matters.

Before the divorce petition can be accepted by the courts and a petition sent out to the other party, it is a standard requirement that both of you attend a MIAM appointment with an approved mediator. In the case of domestic abuse mediation isn't usually possible so in this instance, you request an exempt certificate from the approved mediator.

Once you have your exempt certificate from the mediator, you can then apply for a divorce and this is as simple as completing a form, either online or by post.

My suggestion would be put your reason for divorce as unreasonable behaviour, as this doesn't need the consent of the other party. Even if they have been unfaithful, using this as a reason requires the other party to acknowledge they have been unfaithful. Domestic abuse is still classed as unreasonable behaviour, so it simple and keep to this as your reason.

Once submitted it takes a couple of weeks to process, and the other party will be issued with the petition to either accept or decline.

What happens if the other party doesn't respond to the petition or rejects it?

In circumstances like this, the court can assign someone to hand deliver the petition to ensure they have it and they will then be given so many days to respond.

If they reject the petition, they then have 28 days to submit a defence to the courts, which will then be given to a judge and a hearing will be arranged where the judge will consider what the other party has said and decide from there. I don't feel this is anything to worry about, as if one person says the relationship is over then the relationship is over, so I am sure if it got to that stage, a judge wouldn't force you to remain married.

Once the petition has been accepted, or the other party don't submit a defence in the allocated time, you are then able to apply for a Decree Nisi, which is the second stage of the divorce process.

Once the judge has signed this step off, the final step is applying for your Decree Absolute which is the final stage needed to end your marriage.

Although there are no restrictions on when you can apply for this final step, it is worth considering holding off until financial agreements have been agreed and signed off.

The reason for this, if your ex was to pass away before a financial settlement has been agreed, any assets could be left to whomever they see fit and if you are no longer legally married, it could create an unnecessary problem that could have been avoided. But these are only my recommendations, you need to do what you feel more comfortable with. When I considered my ex's lifestyle and the issues he had experienced medically as a result of these ongoing issues, a drink fuelled accident wasn't out of the realms of possibility, so I chose to hold off from for that reason.

## CHILD ARRANGEMENTS

The next thing I'm going to cover is child arrangements.

No doubt this is the immediate cause of frustration and conflict with the other party. If, however, you are confident they won't attempt to gain access, then you may choose to leave this step alone. However, if there is any possibility they could apply for a child arrangements order via the courts and there are clear safe guarding risks towards you or the children, my advice would be initiate this yourself at your first opportunity. This will allow you to make the courts and CAFCAS s aware of the details surrounding the domestic abuse and any safeguarding concerns you have regarding the children.

There are certainly two schools of thought to the above. Some solicitors and McKenzie friends would say just leave it and see if the other party puts in an application, because that way, it costs them to apply rather than costing you and you're buying yourself time. And although in some ways, I agree, that also brings uncertainty and a feeling of looking over your shoulder, wondering when or if the other parent will make an appearance in the future. I preferred to feel in control of the process.

Another good reason to be the applicant is, it is for the other party to defend the allegations made against them, whereas if he puts the application in, it is on you to disprove any allegations made against you, which is likely to include alienation.

You will, of course, get the opportunity to put your case forward regarding your concerns, but I was very mindful that if I left the process to my ex, then CAFCAS s would have inaccurate facts from the start.

These are just points to keep in mind when considering child arrangements orders, but you have to do what you feel most comfortable with.

The forms you need to complete here are the C100 & C1A which is where you would make the courts and CAFCAS s aware of any history of domestic abuse.

Once you submit your child arrangements order to the court, it will then be passed over to CAFCAS s who will gain contact with you by a secure email portal. This email will come up as NEITGeneric with a banner image of CCAFCAS s in the body of the email. You will also see a link that says read this secure email and you will be prompted to either sign in or register. Please be mindful, if you have used this service in the past via another government network using the email address the courts have on file, you will need to use those past log-in details. If you cannot remember these, click on having problems accessing email link, which you will find in the body of the email, and this will direct you to access support with egress.com.

Egress is the service the government use for all secure emails, and they can easily reset your password for you.

I thought it would be useful to walk you through this process as it was an issue I stumbled across. Any small nuggets of advice that may make this process a little less stressful is always useful.

Once you receive your appointment with CAFCAS s, you will be asked a series of questions around the domestic abuse. These will require you answering either all the time, somewhat, or never.

It really is as black and white as that. There is very little discussion that will take place where you can put your feelings across. They have a script to follow, and they base their report on how you answer the questionnaire, any answers they get back from the other parent, combined with the details provided in the original application and any FACTS that show up in the police checks.

At this stage, medical records and physical evidence isn't looked at, which is the reason I feel so strongly about getting the true facts across to CAFCAS s in the initial application from the start. The information you provide in the initial application and the process CAFCAS s take you through is going to support their recommendations to the courts when it comes to safeguarding checks and access.

It is important to note, solicitors are not able to be present for the appointments with CAFCAS s, however, if you wish to have a McKenzie friend to support you or take notes, this is usually allowed with prior agreement with the CAFCAS s officer.

After the report has been issued to the courts, along with CAFCAS s recommendations, you will be sent a date to attend a child arrangement hearing with a judge. This is when the judge will consider the recommendations the CCAFCAS s officer has made and, depending on what these are, will determine if a fact-finding hearing is required. This is where medical files and any other reports are sourced and provided to the courts.

Some possible outcomes that may be considered where there is evidence of domestic abuse and or safeguarding concerns for the children are:

- Completing a Domestic Abuse Perpetrators Course could be a condition the judge may order before direct access can be approved.
- If there are any issues around substance abuse, then the courts could order the completion of a recovery program and have regular tests to ensure they are clean/ sober for a period before granting direct access.
- Supervised access in a contact centre either with a report or not. These supervised visitations usually come with a cost to the other party.
- Indirect contact, which could include anything from phone

call/ video calls at set times and dates, or even just emails or letters so many times a year.

Gradual unsupervised access leading up to overnight access, again this is usually done at different stages as they monitor how things are between the parent and child. I know the thought of overnight visits or even unsupervised access may fill you with dread, and I totally relate to this concern. But if the judge orders and approves this, you must be seen as encouraging your children to want to spend time with the other parent, otherwise, if the other parent takes the matter back to court, it could be seen as you're not acting in the child's best interest.

But for now, it is important you remain as positive. Utilise all your regulation tools to stay out of the emotional part of your brain. Clear and rational thinking is vital to get the best outcome for you and your children.

You may also want to consider applying for a Non molestation order and/or an Occupational Order.

**Non-Mal** order is an order made by the court to prevent the perpetrator contacting or coming anywhere near you and is enforceable.

**Occupational Order** is an order made by the courts regarding residential rights to any marital home for you and your children whilst awaiting an agreement to be met in the financial side of things.


FINANCES:

When it comes to finances, my suggestion would be writing to your ex or his solicitor and put a WITHOUT PREJUDISE OFFER in the first instance.

This wording is extremely important when making any offers to the other side, regardless of the stage of the process.

Present the without prejudice proposal with an expiry date to accept or come back with a counteroffer, advising them if a suitable agreement cannot be met by the date stated, you will be applying to court for financial settlement.

Ensure you highlight any needs that are primarily to support the immediate needs of the children.

My advice is to follow through on this.

Negotiating with an abuser who has a history of controlling behaviour is a fruitless exercise and will only add to your frustrations and delay things from moving forward. This is another reason avoiding a solicitor to do this for you. Many solicitors will continue to negotiate with an individual who is likely to keep moving the goal posts. It is also highly unlikely that the other party will even take the advice given to them by their representation.

The forms you need to complete are Form A for the initial application.

Once informed by the court of a date, you will then need to complete Form E, which needs to be exchanged with the other party at the same time and submitted to the court by the instructed date. Ideally, the other party have a solicitor representing them so you can agree a date with the solicitor to do this by hand, and no communication needs to take place between the two of you.

If you manage to agree a financial arrangement prior to applying to court, then you would be potentially looking at engaging in a voluntary exchange of Form E prior to this application.

This is very straight-forward but it is highly unlikely any agreements will be met outside of court considering the nature of the individual.

Additionally to Form E, you will be asked to provide the court with:

- a concise statement of apparent issues between you and the other party. This is self-explanatory.
- a Chronology, which is a history of events within the marriage. Things that you would include are:

If you resided together prior to getting married; if so, when?

Date of marriage.

How many children you have?

When the property or other assets were purchased.

This is where you could include any significant events involving domestic abuse -

If you were injured and taken to hospital, or where the police were involved/notified. You will also need to include the date if you have since left the family home; Any Miam appointments that have been attended, which is your appointments with the mediators.

- A questionnaire setting out the further information you require from the other party.

This is particularly important if you need further evidence of any pensions, investments, business accounts or any other assets. Both parties need to be aware of these things to make a final decision on how assets are to be split. Also, whether you have any questions you would like the judge to ask the other party or have them explain based on the information they have provided in the Form E or other disclosures.

It is important to bear in mind, the questionnaire is not an opportunity to question the other side around their requests and expectations around the split of assets, this will be covered in the final hearing.

- Form H is a list of legal costs incurred through the proceedings.

This wouldn't include any costs incurred through a McKenzie friends you consult with, as this is deemed as a private arrangement.

- And finally, a notice of Form G, which is to highlight if either party will be able to proceed with financial resolution and just give a brief reason as to why you will or will not be able ready to come to an arrangement on the first appointment.

The first appointment is to ensure both parties have submitted everything they are required to by the courts. If something hasn't been provided, this is where the judge will give either party a list of tasks to complete by a certain date in the hope that on the next hearing, both parties are able to agree on a settlement.

If both parties can agree on the directions hearing, it is possible to close off on the first appointment with a settlement agreed and signed off, but this is unlikely for many who have experienced any form of financial abuse from the other party.

The family court is an extended opportunity to make life difficult for you, so my advice is to expect the worst and anything better is a bonus.

The second appointment is not dis-similar to the first appointment, where the judge will establish if one or both parties have completed the tasks set out by the judge in the directions hearing. The judge is initially acting as a mediator or middle person so both parties can come to an agreement and act in the best interest of the children. Throughout the hearing, both parties will be able to go away and discuss numbers. If the parties are struggling to agree, this is when the judge will offer his/her opinion. If, however, the judge's opinion isn't suited to either party, this is where it will move to a third hearing, potentially with a different judge. Both parties take the risk of a different judge having a different opinion on how assets should be split.

In the final hearing, the judge will make an outcome on both party's behalf based on the details that have been provided by both parties and what he/she feels is in the best interest of any minors, which will be based on housing needs, capacity to earn and maintain as close to as reasonable lifestyle as before the breakdown of the marriage.

This may go either way for both parties, which is why it is much better trying to come to an arrangement between you. This however is not often possible when dealing with an Ex-partner presenting with Narcissistic traits and behaviours.

## COSTS FOR THE APPLICATIONS

There will certainly be fees that apply for each separate application. Unfortunately, these need to be paid by the applicant despite who is at fault.

If you are receiving benefits or can prove you are on a low income, you could potentially be approved for these costs to be wavered. You submit a request for this online, selecting the appropriate form you want an excemption code for. This is then emailed to you and displayed on screen so you can add the relevant exception code to the form before submitting.

Web address: https://www.gov.uk/get-help-with-court-fees

## CHILD MAINTENANCE

Although this can be discussed through the financial proceedings, it is always better to get this managed by CSA, so maintenance can be addressed sooner rather than later.

If the other parent is refusing to pay maintenance to support their children, I would strongly urge you to give CSA a call. They will discuss the details with you and arrange a call back based on the details provided.

Number: 0800 1712345

You will be emailed a link to complete the application process online where you can expect a response within 6 weeks, once they have tried to gain contact with the other parent.

If the other parent doesn't respond to their letter within 14 days, they will then access their earnings via their NI details and contact their employer directly to have the calculated amount taken out of their wages prior to being paid.

This route does take much longer, so be prepared for this to take a further three months before you start receiving payments for maintenance. This will, however, include any arrears which back dates to the time they first contacted the other parent regarding this new case.

Once a payment has been agreed with the other party, if they miss any payments this can then be reported to CSA once five days have lapsed from the expected date, and CSA will investigate this further.

That gives you a detailed snapshot of the court and finances process from start to finish.

Hopefully you have been reassured that you do not need to have the financial burden of hiring a solicitor to fill out forms - forms a solicitor will give you to complete the best part of anyway.

However, I understand it can all be a little daunting, so if you do need some support navigating your way through this, either contact a McKenzie friend local to you, or alternatively, there is the Family & Civil service line. They offer free court advice and can help with completing forms, either in person or over the phone and can even support you in court just as a Mckenzie friend will.

They are located in the court builds but are not legally trained.

www.supportthroughcourt.org

## WHAT IS A MCKENZIE FRIEND?

A McKenzie friend is there to support and guild a litigant in person through the family court process. They are not legally trained but have gone through detailed training in understanding the dynamics of the different stages of divorce and child arrangement process.

Your McKenzie friend can support you and guild you through completing forms and gathering documents for court, but they cannot complete this on your behalf.

Your McKenzie friend can attend court hearings with you, advise quietly throughout the hearing and take notes on your behalf. If you wish to take a break to consult with your McKenzie friend, you can request this, and the judge will normally accommodate this request, but your McKenzie friend is not able to speak on your behalf.

Unlike a solicitor, your McKenzie friend can attend CAFCAS interviews to take notes if you wish. You just need to advise your CAFCAS officer they will be attending in advance of the appointment.

McKenzie friends do normally charge for their services, although these are significantly less than that of a solicitor.

The aim of a McKenzie friend is to guild you through the admin process of family court, support and advise you in court if needed, but always aiming to keep your costs to a minimum.

**Other useful contacts to have:**

I'm based in Manchester UK and there is a service available at Manchester law school where you can receive free legal advice, via zoom, from a trained solicitor with a law student present. This is only to over guidance; they do not represent anyone through proceedings.

Details for this service are: freelegalhelp@manchester.ac.uk

Also, there is a charity called Advocate that finds free legal assistance from volunteer barristers. There are criteria to meet but certainly worth exploring.

www.weareadvocate.org.uk

If I knew back then what I know now, I would utilise the services with the family & civil service line for the initial process of completing forms because there is no charge for this service.

I would consult a solicitor for specific legal advice around children and finances at the law school in Manchester.

And I would only use a McKenzie friend for support during hearings. Or if finances allowed, I would instruct a solicitor or a direct access at this point if I didn't feel confident speaking on my own behalf in a court setting.

This is by far is the best use of funds.

## REGULATION TIPS FOR COURT

- Keep a bottle of ICE-COLD water, maybe use an insulated flask and place ice cubes into the water. This is useful to sip throughout the hearing to keep the nervous system regulated.
- Scan your surroundings and become aware of your eyeline activation points, and position yourself so your line of vision is intentionally directed to your NON-ACTIVATION line of vision. This will prevent you getting activated unnecessarily.
- Use the Bilateral Breakthrough technique to self-sooth if you feel yourself becoming triggered.

This, along with some gentle tapping is a subtle self-regulation technique which won't bring attention to yourself.

Check in the resource area for both these techniques

https://traumaandanxietybreakthrough.com/**book-resources**/

There are also some useful video resources from legal experts in the resource area.

(All forms are correct at the time of publishing Oct 2021)

---

*"Don't Be Afraid.*

*When You Remain Focused, Determined, Hopeful &*
*Empowered, Success Will Be ours!"*

---

# UNDERSTANDING YOUR ABUSER

*U*nderstanding and accepting the dynamics of your relationship with the abuser is important to begin to break the trauma bond.

Being Narcissism informed, one thing I see people asking a lot is:

## IS MY ABUSER A NARCISSIST?

The simple answer to that question is, it doesn't matter.

ABUSE IS ABUSE, whatever label you attach to your perpetrator. Abuse is unacceptable regardless of the cause or motive and you deserve to be happy and treated respectfully.

Sugar coating this behaviour with a diagnosis doesn't excuse the effect this toxic behaviour has on your wellbeing and that of your children. For years I blamed my husband's behaviour on his excessive drinking, but the truth was I was enabling him.

Enabling is a common term used with loved ones around addiction, but the same applies to those who experience domestic abuse. We enable our abusers, and without consequences, the behaviour continues.

However, it's still beneficial to understand the main traits and characteristics of the main cluster B personality traits, particularly those of a Narcissist.

It is perpetrators with narcissistic traits and behaviours that will have you questioning your own judgement. Having this understanding allows you to see their manipulative mind games, start viewing your relationship for what it is, and stop questioning your own judgement. By understanding your abuser's rules, you can start playing the game differently, ensuring you always remain a step ahead of the narcissist.

Abusers generally fall into one of the cluster B personality types, in my opinion. There are a whole bunch of them, but I just want to show you how characteristics can overlap and why diagnosing is so challenging.

Remember, without an official diagnosis we can't officially say they have NPD (narcissistic personality disorder) , but we can highlight they have Narcissistic tendencies and traits.

If you look at the chart below, you will see sociopaths have very similar traits to a narcissist, as do psychopaths.

Check out the charts below

(These are also in your resource area)

## Comparison Chart

| SOCIOPATH | NARCISSIST | PSYCHOPATH |
|---|---|---|
| Is created through childhood experiences | Is created | Is born this way |
| Emotional | Emotional | Unemotional |
| Inclined to engage in crime | Not inclined to crime | Not inclined to commit crime |
| Feels remorse | Doesn't feel remorse | Doesn't feel remorse |
| Gains pleasure from violent acts | Can be violent | Violence is power |
| Recognises their wrongs | Emotionally shallow / Selfish | Can not recognise right from wrong |
| Emotionally unstable erratic behaviour | Can experience Psychosis | Cold, calculated |
| Experiences psychosis | Passive aggressive | High IQ |
| Low IQ | Rage | Does not experience Psychosis |
| No patience | Recognises other peoples emotions | Patient |
| | Emotionally unstable | Ability to mimic rage and other emotions |
| | Average IQ | |
| | Passive Aggressive | |
| | No patience | |

This is the reason; I want to encourage you not to focus too much on the label and only look at the traits. The more traits they display on a regular basis, the higher the chances are they have NPD.

## Narcissistic Traits
www.traumaandanxietybreakthrough.com

| RELATIONAL | BEHAVIOURAL | ACTIVATIONAL | ANTAGONISTIC | COGNITIVE |
|---|---|---|---|---|
| LACK OF EMPATHY | COERCIVE SARCASTIC | RAGE | ARROGANT SELF CENTRED | LACK OF SELF |
| LYING | CARELESS ADDICTION | ANGER | EXPLOITIVE ARGUMENTATIVE | HYPERSENSITIVE |
| MANIPULATIVE | ENVIOUS CHEATING | INSECURE | NO RESPONSIBILITY STUBBORN | PARANOID |
| PROJECTION | GENEROUS | SHAME | VINDICTIVE | NO GUILT |
| CONTEMPT | CHEAP | IMPULSIVE | COMPETITIVE | NO REMORSE |
| CONTOLLING GASLIGHTING | VICTIM | CHILD LIKE | ENTITLED | JUDGEMENTAL |
| LACK OF BOUNDARIES | SUPERFICIAL SUPERIOR | DISCONNECTED | GRANDIOSE | LACK OF INSIGHT |
| DISMISSIVE JEALOUSY | PESSIMIST | ALONE | PASSIVE AGGRESSIVE | NO RESPONSABILITY |
| | OPTIMIST | | CONDESENDING | |

Looking at some of these behaviours, you may recognise some of these in yourself.

Firstly, we all have some narcissistic traits, but somebody who is bordering on having narcissistic personality disorder wouldn't admit there's anything to fix or heal. Very few individuals with NPD seek support from a therapist. Even if they do engage in therapy, they will most likely manipulate the therapist, which adds a whole other level of complication because a therapist can only diagnose based on the behaviours and traits they witness.

One thing narcissist are masters at is hiding their true self if there is something to be gained from doing so.

Most narcissist's will only engage in therapy as a means of securing their supply.

For example:

If they feel they are losing their grip of you, they will promise you the world to prevent you from leaving. This is only to draw you back into the shared fantasy enough that you remain on the hamster wheel. By hiding their true self with a therapist, this gives them ammunition to throw this back at you:

"It's not me, it is you that is the problem."

All behaviours a Narcissists displays serves a purpose, which is to make them feel powerful and God-like. Only then can they escape the emotional wounds from childhood.

To them, power validates their self-worth, something they won't sacrifice for anything or anyone. This would explain why some psychologists refers to patients who fall into the cluster B personality groups as:

"VERY DIFFICULT PEOPLE."

And boy, is that true.

The other problem when it comes to diagnosing someone who falls into cluster B group is the DSM- 5 doesn't list all the traits.

When a psychologist is diagnosing someone with any personality disorder, it isn't as technical as you would expect.

They look to meet five traits listed in the DSM-5 (**manual for assessing and diagnosing mental health disorders**)

If symptoms happen to overlap different personality traits, or the traits they have are not listed in the DSM, it is unfortunately a case of:

"The computer says YES," or, "The computer says NO"

To quote the words of Professor of Psychology, and self-aware Narcissist Sam Vaknin:

**A narcissist can be aware but never cured!**

Therefore, even if you are lucky enough to get your abuser into therapy, there is no trauma professional in the world that can cure disorders like this.

Sam Vaknin is a self-aware narcissist, and he claims narcissist are very aware of their behaviours and they know how these behaviours impact those around them psychologically. So why is a narcissist so sadistic and manipulative in their ways?

Narcissists and Sociopaths are formed the same way Co-dependents are - due to

childhood emotional experiences that have led to trauma encoding. The cruel and sadistic traits are there as a means of soothing and protecting their inner wounds and that desire to protect those inner wounds is so strong that they detach from emotion towards others.

Emotion equals pain and their system recognises this from a young age, which is why this conditioning is so strong.

It's important to understand that they are not behaving in this way because of you; they would behave like this whoever they were gaining supply from.

Power and control make them feel worthy and they do that by devaluing others and moving them into a place of fear.

Fear is where they have most control.

Fear is their number one weapon in a quest to feel powerful and in control of their own life and their own emotions. They don't ever want to feel or experience past emotional experiences from childhood.

You may think your abuser can show empathy towards others and they may easily get upset. It is all an act to make you feel sorry for them when they feel they have overstepped the mark. If they feel they are losing their grip of you and the situation, they can switch on empathy and remorse remarkably well. But understand this is fake and a way of manipulating you. Empathy isn't something that comes naturally to them. They can put on an Oscar winning performance, but don't buy it.

Even if they are threatening to end their own life, this is a manipulation tactic to draw you back in using your empathic nature. A narcissist will use your good and bad qualities to their own advantage.

Firstly, most don't have the guts to end their life. The whole intention is to get a reaction and secure supply in the form of sympathy from others.

If nothing else, they will want to stick around to reap the rewards for their performance.

Although, their dramatics can go too far on occasions, please remember they are grown adults and you are not responsible for them. The best way to deal with this is to not give them a direct response, just call the police/ambulance and let them attend to the matter.

The important thing is to keep yourself and your children safe.

Think of your relationship as a cult and HE is the leader of this cult. Within any cult they groom and mould you into the person they need you to be. The minute you step out of line, be under no illusions, any fake emotion they pretended to have for you will very quickly turn to anger and hate.

## SO HOW THE HECK DID YOU GET INTO THIS STICKY MESS?

We talk about this in more detail when we dig into your younger self, but in a nutshell, it is all as a result of your conditioning from childhood and your lack of self-worth.

Looking at this from your abuser's perspective, it all starts with love bombing, as the narcissist says all the right things and behaves like the perfect gentleman. They are your knight in shining armour, swooping in to rescue the princess. This is exactly how he wants you to feel.

He just gets you!

Your body feels that "feel good" rush of dopamine, oxytocin and serotonin and you are on cloud nine.

The narcissist identifies very quickly you suffer with what's known as Cinderella syndrome, so all their behaviours are designed to draw you in, hook, line and sinker!

The narcissists will use this love bombing stage to pick out any insecurities you have, making you feel heard and listened to, intentionally making you feel you can trust them. You open up and reveal all your deepest and darkest secrets.

Now that they have you hooked, this is when the devaluing stage creeps in, and the mask starts to slip.

You start to notice the toxic traits appear, one by one.

At first, you dismiss them as them having a bad day.

Then, you start to think you imagined it all.

Until one day, they have you blaming yourself.

Anger and the name calling usually starts as you question any of their outbursts, question why they may be withdrawing love or intimacy. Sex is often used as a tool - either you get lots of it to make you feel loved and adored, or they withdraw sex completely. Sex is a way of controlling you.

Now you're on an endless quest to find the person you fell in love with, the man who loved you unconditionally in the beginning.

And because we are so afraid of never finding that again, we, as co-dependents, fight tooth and nail to get that back.

After marriage or children is when this usually starts because this is when it is more difficult for you to escape the fantasy and a whole load more self-belief wounds come up for you:

I don't want to be a single parent.

You stay married, no matter what.

I've got to stay for the kids.

No contact, or extreme modified contact, is the only effective way to start to break the trauma bond. Being in a trauma bonding is a form of addiction and, like any addict, you need to wean off the habit.

## ABANDONING A NARCASIST

This is probably the worst thing you could do to a narcissist. It reopens their childhood abandonment wounds.

This is when they are at their most dangerous.

Abandonment doesn't always come in the form of physically leaving them, although that is the most common way. Narcissists do not respond well if the person they are getting their narcissistic supply from becomes seriously unwell, or their supply's life suddenly becomes at risk for some reason.

You see, the narcissist doesn't rationalise you may not be abandoning them through choice.

All they see is that you are rubbing salt into that already gaping wound from childhood and they will punish you for this.

A narcissist will never punish you at the detriment of their reputation. Although behind closed doors they may bring the devil in them out to play, as soon as they step out into society, this is where the fake empathy makes an appearance, and the crocodile tears start to flow.

## NARCASISTS AND SPECIAL OCCASIONS

Have you ever wondered why special occasions are always ruined?

Birthdays, Christmas, Anniversaries, Mother's Day, even holidays?

This is no coincidence. A narcissist hates not being centre of attention, their brain just cannot cope with it. By causing a scene, they very conveniently shift the attention back to them, either in the form of negative attention or by causing people to pander around them, working hard to ease the atmosphere they have created.

I'm hoping you have some more things to add to your list of reasons to heal from this point. Imagine, Christmas without an atmosphere, enjoyable birthday celebrations!

## THINGS TO KNOW WHEN LEAVING A NARCASIST

1) the person you fell in love with does not exist. It was a fantasy they drew you into.

2) Don't worry about what they are telling everyone else. If there is one thing I am sure of, the Narcissist is great at playing the victim. They will most likely be blaming you for the breakdown of the relationship.
What they won't be telling anyone is all the times they lied, cheated, bullied, blackmailed and gaslighted you, when all the time they were the one who engaged in controlling and coercive behaviour for the best part of the relationship.

3) Remember your worth, which is everything this book is about. You selflessly loved them despite all the abuse, but they never deserved your loyalty.
Now is the time to turn that loyalty towards yourself and your children

4) Be prepared for them to weaponise and even punish the children.
They may even discard the children.
Remember, this has nothing to do with the children but everything to do with you.
Your abuser has lost control of you, so they will control you the only way they can and that's via the children and finances.

## REMEMBER THE RED FLAGS OF ABUSE

- Embarrassing or putting you down.
- Looking at you or acting in ways that scare you.
- Controlling who you see, where you go, or what you do.
- Keeping you from, or discouraging you from, seeing your friends or family.
- Taking your money or refusing to give you money for expenses.
- Preventing you from making your own decisions.
- Telling you that you are a bad parent or threatening to harm or take away your children.
- Preventing you from working or attending school.
- Blaming you for the abuse, or acting like it's not really happening.
- Destroying your property or threatening to hurt or kill your pets.
- Intimidating you with guns, knives, or other weapons.
- Shoving, slapping, choking or hitting you.
- Attempting to stop you from pressing charges.
- Threatening to commit suicide because of something you've done.
- Giving you the silent treatment.
- Threatening to kill you.
- Pressuring you to have sex when you don't want to, or do things sexually that you're not comfortable with.
- Pressuring you to use drugs or alcohol.
- Preventing you from using birth control or pressuring you to become pregnant when you're not ready.
- Be aware of how they treat other people - do they speak disrespectfully to others or about others.
- Declaring their undying love for you quickly, frequently and publicly (e.g., on social media).
- Trying to get you to dress the way they want you to,

## TWENTY COMMON TERMS REFERRED TO IN NARCISSISTIC ABUSE

### 1. Love Bombing

Love bombing is a term used to describe the initial stage of a relationship.

This is where the narcissist goes all out to impress you. They will make promises for the future that lights up your heart.

### 2. Boundaries

Boundaries are a set of rules which we consider to be reasonable behaviours and expectations from those around us. Narcissists never respect boundaries and will get angry if you try to enforce these on them. This is how you disconnect with who you are and your values, and you disconnect with what's important to you in life.

### 3. Gas-lighting

Gas-lighting is a manipulative tactic where a mentally healthy individual is subjected to conditioning so that they doubt their own sanity or even agree to things that they know may be morally or even legally wrong. You may start to believe that your perception of reality is false. The narcissist may deny saying something or pretend something they have done hasn't happened. Over time, you start to feel confused or maybe even think you are going crazy.

### 4. Enabler

An enabler is someone who, by their action or lack of action, encourages or enables a pattern of behaviour to continue, or removes consequences for bad behaviour. This is also a common term used with those supporting loved ones through addictions.

### 5. Flying Monkeys

Flying monkeys are people who have been convinced by the narcissist that he or she is the real victim. They inflict further harm on the real victim by submitting to the narcissist's wishes and demands. They may threaten, torment, and discredit you in any way they see fit by spreading lies and gossip.

## 6. Grey Rock

Grey rock is a term used to describe your behaviour when trying to cut contact with a narcissist. The aim is to be utterly boring so that the narcissist no longer sees you as good supply and subsequently disappears.

## 7. Hoovering

The term, hoovering describes how a narcissist attempts to suck their victims back into a relationship. They will use every trick in the book to get you back under their control. They often promise to change their behaviour, or say they cannot live without you.

Mine even said I should divorce him and if I did, he would give me and our daughter everything.

## 8. Reactive Abuse

A narcissist loves to provoke a reaction from you. They will provoke you into responding in an angry or often irrational manner. This response validates your unbalanced state of mind and is great for deflecting attention away from their toxic behaviour with you and others.

## 9. Mirroring

A narcissist will mirror what they see in you, from your mannerisms, to your likes and dislikes. They basically become exactly what you want them to be to have you feel that soulmate connection. Likewise, the one being victimised, or even children being exposed to abuse in the home, can mirror the behaviours of the abuser as a survival tactic. This when the one being abused will question if they are in fact the narcissist, but often these behaviours are being mirrored to keep you safe.

## 10. Narcissistic Supply

A narcissist is lost without narcissistic supply. Supply consists of attention, admiration, respect, even fear. Without these things being fed to them consistently, the narcissist will become dysfunctional.

## 11. No Contact

No contact is put in place by a victim in order to give themselves time to recover. It is not, in any way, like the narcissist's silent treatment. A narcissist who initiates the silent treatment is doing so as a punishment and to exert power and control.

No contact is a self-imposed set of rules whereby there will be no contact with the toxic person (no texts, no emails, no phone calls, no snooping on social media). It has been likened to building a wall between you and a toxic individual. You will not care or even be aware of what happens on the other side of this wall. (Minimal contact is advised in circumstances where one must co-parent with a narcissist).

## 12. Projection

A narcissist is an expert at projecting their own flaws or bad behaviour onto others. They will never hold themselves accountable for any wrongdoing and will blame others for the very things that they do themselves. The main objective is to make themselves feel superior.

You may notice they will accuse a friend or colleague of doing the very things they are guilty of.

## 13. Scapegoat

The scapegoat is blamed for just about everything that goes wrong. A child in a family may be singled out and subjected to unwarranted negative treatment.

## 14. Trauma Bonding

Trauma bonding is a misplaced loyalty where a victim is emotionally bonded with their abuser and finds themselves unable to leave an unhealthy or dangerous relationship. The victim remains loyal to someone who has betrayed them repeatedly throughout most of their relationship.

## 15. Self Esteem

Self-esteem is the overall judgement one holds about their own self-worth, which would include pride in oneself, self-respect and self-assurance.

## 16. Triangulation

Narcissists thrive on chaos. They provoke rivalry and jealousy between people, creating triangles in order to boost their own ego.

## 17. Closure

Closure in a normal relationship involves honest communication about what has gone happened and you both move on. After a relationship with a narcissist, the person who has experienced the abuse leaves with so many questions unanswered. We cannot expect any form of closure from the emotionally unavailable narcissist, who is completely lacking in empathy, with no regard for your feelings. The only closure in this type of relationship is the closure you give yourself by accepting that what you thought you had was never real.

---

**"Leave The Person Who Hurt You in The Past,**

**But Never Forget the Lessons They Taught You."**

---

# IMPLEMENTING HEALTHY BOUNDARIES

*B*oundaries are not something a co-dependant is good at enforcing, particularly in a romantic setting. Once an abuser draws you into the fantasy, they have you hooked. We quickly lose sight of what our boundaries and values were prior to the relationship.

Boundaries should be there to take care of ourselves and respect our feelings.

If your abuser has narcissistic characteristics, it is most likely they have slowly moulded you into the person they want you to be. Be under no illusions, they have been incredibly subtle in doing so. The moment your guard is down, they slowly change the rules and your eagerness to please has you moulded into the obedient little wife/partner they need/want you to be.

You become a slave to their ego. And their ego is their lifeline.

Re-connecting with your values and starting to implement small but safe boundaries during the exit process is a vital part of healing. When you understand how to set and maintain healthy boundaries, you can avoid future feelings of resentment, disappointment, and anger that build up when limits have been pushed.

## SO, WHAT ARE BOUNDARIES AND VALUES?

When you define your personal values, you discover what's truly important to you. A good way of starting to do this is to look back on your life prior to meeting your current partner and identify when you felt good and confident that you were making good choices.

Boundaries can take many forms. They can range from being rigid and strict to appearing almost non-existent.

If you have more rigid boundaries, you might:

- keep others at a distance,
- seem detached, even with intimate partners,
- have few close relationships,
- avoid close relationships.

When your boundaries are more relaxed, you may:

find you get too involved with other people's problems,

- find it difficult to say "no" to others',
- be guilty of oversharing personal information.
- seek to please others for fear of rejection.

And these are all classic traits of someone who is co-dependent.

A person with healthy boundaries understands that making their expectations clear helps to establishes what behaviour you will accept from other people, and it establishes what behaviour other people can expect from you.

When you have healthy boundaries, you will:

- start to share personal information appropriately (not too much, or not too little),

- understand your personal needs and wants and know how to communicate them,
- value your own opinions but accept when others may not agree with you.

Many of us have a mix of boundaries depending on the situation. For example, you might have strict boundaries at work and more relaxed boundaries at home or with family and friends.

Often culture can influence someone's boundaries and values.

Some cultures find that sharing personal information is not appropriate at any time, while in other cultures, sharing might be encouraged. But when it comes to values and boundaries brought about by cultural beliefs, it is important to truthfully ask yourself, are these YOUR BELIFS or have those beliefs been conditioned into you?

If they have been conditioned, this can be a form of abuse that is hidden behind cultural beliefs, which is very common in many religious families.

## TYPES OF BOUNDARIES

Building healthy boundaries — whether you're at work, at home, or hanging out with friends — hinges on understanding the types of boundaries.

**Physical Boundaries:**

This refers to your personal space, your privacy, and your body.

Are you comfortable with public displays of affection (hugs, kisses, and handholding), or do you find these displays of affection intrusive?

**Sexual Boundaries:**

These are your expectations concerning intimacy.

Sex is a favourite weapon of choice for a narcissist, in that they will either use sex to love bomb and make you feel desirable and wanted, or they will withdraw sex to punish and assert 'their control.

Sexual comments and touching inappropriately might make you feel uncomfortable.

### Intellectual Boundaries:

These boundaries concern your thoughts and beliefs. Intellectual boundaries are not respected when someone dismisses another person's ideas and opinions.

### Emotional Boundaries:

This refers to a person's feelings. You might not feel comfortable sharing your feelings about everything with a friend or partner. Instead, you prefer to share gradually over time.

### Financial Boundaries:

This one, as you guessed, is all about money. Financial control is something that is common in an abusive relationship.

Maybe you like to save for the future

Maybe you believe we only live once so money should be spent to bring joy to your life.

Maybe financial freedom and independence is something that's important to you.

When you get ready to establish your boundaries, be sure to take each one of the above into account.

I am sure you can identify something in each of these where the abuser in your life has not considered your feelings on several occasions.

## THE LOWDOWN ON PERSONAL BOUNDARIES

In a nutshell, it's knowing how to separate your feelings from someone else's. As human beings, we have our own thoughts, memories, and lived experiences, and sometimes, that can become very blurred with someone else's. No more so than those of an abuser, where we mirror their behaviours and beliefs as a way of self-protection.

Our brain wants only to keep us safe, so by mirroring your abuser and conforming to how they want you to be, do and act, the brain thinks it is safer than the potential rejection.

But this is where the internal war occurs.

Boundaries are healthy for helping you maintain your identity and feel safe by honouring and respecting yourself.

When we disrespect our boundaries and values, our system doesn't feel safe, and the panic system is activated. Therefore, we are in a constant state of dis regulation.

An example of this is when my ex-husband rang me up to say he was in trouble at work because his boss had found out about an inappropriate message sent to a woman on his LinkedIn account. He and I knew he did it, but he was insistent someone hacked his account, and his boss wanted a name. Because he didn't have a name, he said I had to take the blame and when I tried to enforce my boundaries, not appreciating being made the scapegoat, he proceeded to gaslight me, suggesting if he lost his job, it would be my fault and our daughter would suffer as a result of me.

Therefore, I disrespected my boundaries through fear of him exposing one of my bigger fears, which was my daughter suffering in any way.

Although I acted from a place of safety, because I had disrespected my own boundaries around this matter, my system still felt dis-regulated because I agreed to something I knew was an injustice.

Setting boundaries is beneficial for far more than just defining our identity. Having boundaries in place limits your exposure to symptoms of anxiety and the body being flooded with cortisol and other stress hormones

Boundaries protect our mental well-being.

## HERE ARE SOME WAYS TO SET AND MAINTAIN GOOD BOUNDARIES.

Start to reflect on past boundaries and values prior to your current relationship.

To successfully introduce and set boundaries, it's important to understand why they're each important to you and how they will benefit your emotional well-being and your life in general.

Start to get curious at the behaviours and traits of your abusive partner and honestly ask yourself how these behaviours make you feel and what needs to change for you to feel respected?

Start small with your boundaries, particularly if you are still living with your abusive partner.

Starting by enforcing boundaries that are too big could put your safety at risk. Once you are safely away, you can start to build on these. No contact or limited contact is a very strong and important boundary when dealing with any abuser moving forward.

Make your boundaries clear early on in future relationships. Sometimes, it can be hard to start putting boundaries in, especially in existing relationships. If you can put in boundaries straight away, it's a lot easier to work with. By setting boundaries and expectations from the very beginning, everyone knows where they stand, and feelings of hurt, confusion, and frustration can be lessened.

Be consistent with boundaries.

Letting boundaries slide can lead to confusion and encourage new expectations and demands among those around you. You will notice, children take advantage when we operate inconsistent boundaries. Equally, in the workplace. If you are a people pleaser in work, you may be inclined to agree to extended hours, when in fact, this doesn't fit in with your family life.

## CREATE A ROUTINE

Consider setting some time to focus on your own self-development and healing, even just 15 minutes in the morning, and ensuring the kids are in bed asleep by a set time.

Giving yourself that time to gather your thoughts and focus on you is not selfish, it is essential.

In some aspects of our lives, there are boundaries already in place — such as in the workplace - but consider these the minimum. Colleagues will likely have some of their own in place, and it's okay for you to add some too.

## BE AWARE OF SOCIAL MEDIA

These platforms allow for more communication than ever, but they've also encouraged some considerable boundary blurring and it is far too easy to get drawn into arguments and debates that leave you feeling overwhelmed and frustrated.

If you deem a particular action as boundary-crossing in real life, your concerns are no less valid when it occurs digitally. You don't have to expose yourself to things on social media that you may find triggering. Next time you read something you disagree strongly with, scroll on by. It will be hard to start with, but your life will be so much more peaceful by steering clear of opinions you can't control.

## BE YOUR BIGGEST CHAMPION

For boundaries to have a strong foundation, you need to show yourself a bit of love. If you've got a belief in your head that says you're worthless and undeserving, then you're going to find it difficult to put boundaries in place that protect your values. This is where the inner child healing comes in on the next chapter.

Gain some perspective. Gaining a healthy balance around boundaries is also important. Having boundaries is important but don't be dictated by them. Sometimes, you've got to go with your gut instinct and occasionally let something go.

Use your intuition; your gut instinct is never wrong.

In addition to setting your own boundaries, it's important to appreciate those of others, even if they're different from your own.

Often, identifying other people's boundaries is about applying common sense. If your partner hates using social media, there's a good chance they won't want those coupled-up selfies plastered across your Instagram or Facebook account. Or, if a friend says they don't want to see a particular movie, don't pester them until they cave in.

This is an example of it being safe to let something that's important you slide.

But repeatedly violating your boundaries and values, can breed resentment and contempt, and cause people to withdraw. This is often where a compromise needs to be met so each party feels like their opinions matter.

Unfortunately, when dealing with narcissists compromises are not possible.

## YOUR TASK TO COMPLETE:

1) Make a list of your top 10 Values.

Think about what's important to you.

If you could wave a magic wand, how would you want your life to be now and in the future.

What do you believe needs to happen for those values to be met?

Here are some more pointers:

- Identify the times when you were happiest.

Find examples from both your career and personal life. This will create balance in your answer.

What were you doing?

Were you with other people? Who?

What other factors contributed to your happiness?

- Identify the times when you were most proud.

Use examples from your career and personal life.

Why were you proud?

Did other people share your pride? Who?

What other factors contributed to your feelings of pride?

- Identify the times when you were most fulfilled and satisfied.

Again, use both work and personal examples.

What need or desire was fulfilled?

How and why did the experience give your life meaning?

What other factors contributed to your feelings of fulfilment?

- Prioritise your top 5 values.

Start with 5 but if you have more, add those to the list.

For example, my values include:

- Maintaining my health.
- Time and financial freedom to live life on my terms and create amazing memories with my daughter.
- Living my purpose to help others to live their best life.
- Putting my daughter back into private school so her educational and emotional needs are met.
- Owning a home outright.

When making decisions, consider does this move me closer to fulfilling what is important to me?

Does a particular decision support how you want to feel?

By prioritising these values, one cannot be achieved without the other.

And these values can alter as you grow and develop.

2) Make a list of 5 small boundaries you can start to implement now with your abusive partner that may start to make life feel a little more tolerable and make you feel that little bit more respectful of yourself.

3) Make a list of boundaries you could start to introduce with family and friends or even work.

4) Make a future list of more firm boundaries for any future partners and, of course, future boundaries to implement with existing relationships.

Remember, baby steps and don't try move mountains too quickly. Slow and steady wins the race, but remaining consistent and revisiting your Values and Boundaries is a good thing to do from time to time, to make sure you're keeping on track.

https://traumaandanxietybreakthrough.com/book-resources/

---

*"Our Boundaries Are a True Reflection of The Respect We Give Ourself, And How We Respect Ourselves Is How We Teach Others to Respect Us."*

---

# HEALING YOUR YOUNGER SELF

Co-dependency and Trauma bonding - what is it and how has it led you to a string of toxic relationships?

Co-dependency is our lack of self-worth, usually formed in childhood. As adults we look to others to fill a void we are unable to fulfil ourselves:

Self-love

Self-respect

Self-care

Self-worth

Self- belief

Notice the repeated word SELF. As a co-dependent, we lack a sense of SELF.

Throw our association of love into the equation, this is the perfect recipe for attracting toxic relationships and friendships into our world.

You likely are not consciously aware your unconscious association with love is negative, particularly as most co-dependent women grow up with Cinderella syndrome.

I'm going to give you a couple of examples so you can maybe start to connect the dots and establish what your interpretation of love is.

Example 1:

Take a child who has grown up with parents who also have a toxic relationship. Maybe they have been exposed to lots of arguments, maybe physical and mental abuse towards one parent.

This child then grows up associating abuse with love.

Example 2:

Take a child who was criticised a lot and felt like they could never do anything right.

This child will grow up associating criticism and disrespect with love.

Although both these situations are unpleasant for anyone to keep experiencing, the brain takes comfort in familiarity; familiarity equals certainty, and certainty equals safety.

Growing up, I was never interested in a boyfriend who treated me respectfully.

Maybe you can relate with the attraction to a bad boy?

Even still, my brother reminds me of the boy I dated briefly when I was living in Dublin, who I split up with because he was too nice.

If truth be known, at the time, I didn't know why I split up with him. All I knew was I didn't feel that excitement.

Today, looking at it through a trauma informed lense he was too nice and to my traumatised system, that was unfamiliar and unfamiliar territory resulted in uncertainty.

All I had ever wanted was to feel loved and accepted, but my whole life I only associated drama and chaos with love.

Of course, my parents loved each other and were always there to support one another, but they argued what felt like constantly, and there was so much disrespect.

I remember Mum storming out of the house in a strop.

Me running after her down the street.

I was exposed to chaos and drama my whole life.

And then, in a blink of an eye everything was rosy again.

This was what my system associated with love.

An abundance of what I thought was loyalty, mixed in with some gaslighting and reactive abuse, emotional blackmail. The silent treatment was another favourite in our household.

Anything outside of these fluctuating behaviours was unfamiliar to my system, therefore, the safest option was to abandon ship and seek out familiar territory.

This is where our trauma bond begins.

Our system becomes addicted to the abuse cycle very early on without us even realising it. Yo-yoing up and down the emotional regulatory ladder becomes a part of life.

Regulated and calm is not something a co-dependent is familiar with.

As we exit one abuse cycle, we enter another, until we heal the wounds from childhood where we developed this association to love.

The brain craves dopamine like an addict craves their choice of drug. In fact, it is Dopamine that is released when any substance is induced, and it is Dopamine that we develop the addiction to, not the source. Therefore, to heal co-dependency and break the trauma bond, like any addict, we first must break the habit. Replacing the source of dopamine with an alternative that's not destructive to us will help to regulate the nervous system. This is where daily implementation of your regulation tools is essential.

But it is only by having awareness of when and how this dependency occurred can we start to heal and break the cycle moving forward.

You may in fact find you have other addictions which act as soothing and numbing out the emotional triggers from the Trauma bond. This could be anything from food to drink or drugs. I talk more about this in emotional band aids, but these also are a product of the root cause. Therefore, we address each dependency with the same set of tools: Condition the system to feel SAFE and de-encode the snapshots taken from early events that are embedded on the fear centre.

Can you see how your abuser is not the cause of your distress? They are more the catalyst that exposed an original wound.

However, your experience with your abuser will have created its own snapshots, due to the altered landscape.

## WHAT ARE SOME OF THE OTHER CHARACTERISTICS OF A CO-DEPENDANT?

- No relationship with ourselves.

What is your self-care like? How often to you do things just to make yourself feel good?

Often a co-dependent is more concerned about doing everything for the benefit of others. Again, this is down to the burdens we carry from childhood associated with our self-belief wounds:

I must be perfect to receive love.

I must make everyone else happy to be worthy of love.

I must be successful to be seen.

I MUST... I MUST... I MUST.

Co-dependants are the proverbial people pleaser. That burden has been a weight we have carried for so long, we forget it is there.

- Do you get accused of gossiping or busy-bodying in people's business?

This serves two purposes in us:

Firstly, if we can fix other people's problems, we might just get the praise and recognition we are longing for.

And the second reason, it stops us focusing on our own problems.

If, by focusing our attention on fixing other people's problems, it results in recognition and praise, it provides our nervous system with the feeling of enough-ness which, is enough to sooth our system long enough until we can get our next dose of breadcrumbs.

Relating this back to relationships, I have had two relationships where they both had serious addiction issues and it gave me something to focus on - if I could FIX them, rescue them, in a way, then surely, I would have earned the right to their love and approval.

Then, maybe I would feel good enough.

This is music to a narcissist's ear, to have the nurturing, ever-pleasing Co-dependant pandering to them and massaging their ego in a desperate attempt to feel good enough.

- Denial.

This is a big one for co-dependents, particularly when it comes to toxic relationships.

A lot of this comes from not wanting to feel like a failure, so we make excuses for bad behaviour until eventually, the burden gets too much to bear and the cracks start to show.

Walking away is not a sign of weakness or failure. Walking away is a sign of strength, healing and self-worth.

- No belief in ourselves, or a fear of abandonment and rejection.

Ironically the very thing we are afraid of is the very thing we associate with love.

- Compulsive behaviour.

This can be anything from making risky financial decisions to dangerous or risky activities.

- Lying or being secretive.

This is done often to hide the fact that we don't feel good enough, or to avoid people seeing us as a failure. A basic example of this is lying about how wonderful your relationship is. If you share the truth, then they may judge your choices or even blame you. All of which exposes those self-belief wounds.

We can become so good at pretending our life is a certain way to others we start to believe our own lies. Maybe you remember being made to keep secrets as a child.

- Most co-dependents find it incredibly hard to trust anyone, not even themselves.

This is another characteristic that can keep us trapped in the abusive cycle. Afraid to trust anyone enough to speak out, afraid to trust ourselves and our own strength to walk away, knowing we will be

OK. Part of my conditioning from a child was, if anyone offered help or support, my programming would be defaulted to expect them to let me down. Even if it meant burn out, I would do everything myself.

- Co-dependants have a need to control their surroundings.

This has always been a big one for me. Because we walk through life expecting others to let us down, this strengthens our need to control situations and outcomes.

As a controlling co-dependent, having solicitors making a long-drawn-out divorce process even more long and drawn-out by trying to negotiate with an unreasonable person, was absolute torture for me. Therefore, apart from the fact you don't need a solicitor to milk you dry of tens of thousands of pounds that you likely don't have going spare, representing yourself, even through the administration side of this, will eliminate so many frustrations and relieve some of those wounds from being exposed whilst you navigate your way through the healing process to become more resilient.

- Co-dependents tend to carry a lot of shame and guilt.

Maybe you were made to feel guilty as a form of punishment as a child?

- It's not uncommon for co-dependants to indulge in alcohol, drugs or even food and shopping as a means of self-soothing.

Unless we are aware, we are unable to heal and if we don't heal, we are likely to repeat the toxic cycle. This is important, not just for yourself, but you also need to break this cycle for your children. These cycles have an uncanny way of repeating themselves generationally.

Have a think about your parent's childhood. How has their upbringing shaped the way they behave as adults? Look at your grandparents.

You will start to notice a generational pattern appear that has ended with you and your children. The good news is, you are choosing to heal and break that cycle so you can live the rest of your life free from these emotional burdens.

Hopefully your children are young enough that your change in direction can move their belief systems to a position of compassion, curiosity, and self-love.

## COMPLEX POST TRAUMATIC STRESS DISORDER

CPTSD is often experienced by people who have experienced domestic abuse and childhood distress, but is often misdiagnosed as Bipolar disorder. The symptoms and traits are identical in that both have you yo-yoing up and down the emotional regulatory ladder, feeling an extreme range of emotions:

INTENSE HAPPINESS

INTENSE RAGE

DEEP DEPRESSION

Due to the fluctuation in emotions, our nervous system is conditioned, from an early age, to believe that these feelings are normal and a way of life. We are already addicted to the abuse cycle from childhood.

I know, looking back at my childhood, I had lots of happy moments which pushed me up to the top of the ladder. But equally, I had many experiences that got my heart racing, feeling like I needed to protect my parents from each other, or even themselves, through the endless arguments I would witness or be brought into the middle of. And many occasions I felt disconnected from the world both at home and at school.

There were even two occasions where our house was broken into, and I remember on both of those occasions, being scared to go to the bathroom at night.

My system was so conditioned to the fight flight freeze cycle, it was the norm.

## YOUNGER SELF COACHING TASKS:

These exercises help us achieve SELF-LOVE, SELF-SUFFICIENCY AND SELF-WORTH.

These are all things we need to be able to give ourselves and lower our expectation of others.

- Access the resources and complete your family tree download and your co-dependency check list. Think about how these traits and characteristics have shaped your life.
- Create a timeline of events, starting from your earliest memory to the current day.

These events should include any unpleasant or traumatic experiences, as well as happy and positive events. As you connect with each event, I want you to think about the emotions you felt at the time and what belief you connected to that event? e.g., I am not good enough, I am a failure, I am worthless, I am not loveable.

The reason for positive and negative events is, I want to start introducing dual thinking. I will cover this in an information processing exercise I'll cover with you in the resource area.

What was the burden you connected to this belief (I must be perfect; I must fix everyone; I must be successful; I must keep the peace)?

Don't worry too much if there are windows in your life you cannot recall, this can happen when our hippocampus shrinks and our capacity in our long-term memory becomes overloaded, causing brain fog and disassociation. As we start to address events, this will make room in the long-term memory and the hippocampus will increase in size. As this happens, you may find memories of past events start coming back to you. As things come back, write them down or make a voice note for yourself so you can come back to it later.

- To understand how your capacity to cope may be influencing your emotional responses towards your kids or other people, take each of the events you have on your timeline, and scale each event as small, medium and large trauma.

Think of these events as marbles being dropped into your brain and, as each of these unprocessed events get added to your long-term memory, capacity exceeds causing an explosion of emotions, brain fog and forgetfulness.

**SEE THE IMAGE BELOW THAT ILLUSTRATES THIS.**

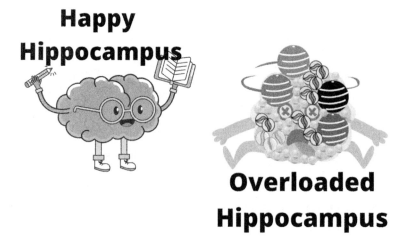

**Happy Hippocampus**

**Overloaded Hippocampus**

Go to your resource area. There is a downloadable visual to start to see how overloaded your capacity could be.

Our goal is to time stamp these events in order to increase our capacity to cope. We do this by accessing the fear centre where these events leave behind biological markers that sit rigidly on the fear centre waiting to be alerted of potential danger. Only by slowing the frequency the brain operates at can we create enough plasticity to communicate with the fear centre and change the response process initiated within our body. This event processing system then frees up space in our long-term memory, which is when we notice the brain fog starting to dissipate and memory starting to return as the hippocampus starts to expand and improve your capacity to cope.

I describe it as gaining a bounce-back ability.

Healing is not about walking through life without a care in the world. Healing enables you to acknowledge without the bodily experience, acknowledging something is challenging and addressing the matter with a clear head.

- Now go back to your timeline of events and check in on your family tree and get curious about what could have influenced certain behaviours to develop.

Understand that although people may have behaved a certain way to you, it was in no way BECAUSE of you.

Get curious about your own behaviours towards others and how they may impact how others feel.

We all respond based on our conditioning from their past events.

- One more exercise I would like you to do to help you pin down your self-belief wounds.

**Ask yourself the following questions:**

If you woke up tomorrow morning and you had your dream life, what would that look like? Where would you be living? What would your house look like? Who is with you? What sort of things are you doing/how are you spending your time? What person are you?

Then ask yourself, if you woke up tomorrow morning and all this was your reality, what do you believe would go wrong?

How would that make you feel?

How would that effect your life and your relationships then?

What's the worst that could happen?

If this devastating outcome was to play out, what would that say about you? Why do you believe this always happens to you?

And finally, what do you believe other people are thinking about you when things go terribly wrong?

Hopefully, after completing these exercises, you're a bit clearer on what your specific self-belief wounds are and what activates the nervous system to respond as it is doing.

So now, I want you to start putting that doubt into question, and to give you an idea of what I mean I'm going to give you a couple of examples:

EXAMPLE ONE: I'm invisible. Nobody is interested in what I share.

This was one of my personal limiting beliefs.

"Really Kate, nobody is interested in what you have to say?"

I would then list the people who genuinely acknowledge the value I share, so that I put that belief into question. Then, I would dig deeper and have my younger self question that belief.

I would think about different times in the past where people were genuinely interested in what I had to share.

Next, ask yourself is there another belief that's influencing this?

Continuing to use my example:

I believed I was a failure and that If I wasn't successful, I wasn't worthy of been heard or seen.

So, I would look to my younger self and acknowledge all my accomplishments as a child!

This exercise is very much about putting our negative beliefs into question as both your adult self and your younger self.

Always remember, it is the younger self that's driving all these emotions and beliefs, which is why it isn't enough just to put those beliefs into question in the here and now. That little girl must start to see her worth and put her story into question.

EXAMPLE TWO: "NOBODY LIKES ME"

Are you sure nobody likes you?

List all the people with whom you have formed a healthy personal or even professional relationship and the connection is genuine.

Do the same with your younger self, recall all your genuine friendships.

This is a good journaling exercise for you.

- Nervous System awareness based on your self-belief wounds you have uncovered:

We looked at the emotional regulation ladder when understanding and getting to know how our children are feeling, and the same thing applies to ourselves.

Look at the LADDER and think about how you feel at each stage of the regulation ladder.

What events or circumstances drop you into fight/flight, and what drops you into freeze or fawn?

Fawn is when we are submissive or pandering to people to smooth the waters.

But more importantly, I want you to start to think about what you need to happen to bring your system back to the top of the ladder into safety?

And then, as I go through the various emotional band aids in the next chapter, think about which band aids are part of your emotional first aid box and where are you on this emotional regulatory ladder for your brain to grant you permission to indulge in such activities.

Remember, although our brain is responding to soothe, the consequences can be devastating, not just for ourselves, but for those around us.

Awareness is an important part of the healing journey. With awareness comes change and growth.

The other thing I want you to become aware of is, where in your body do you FEEL certain emotions?

Some examples are I feeling anger in the tummy, I feel sadness in the heart.

These are very personal to you, so really connect with all the emotions and beliefs you have become aware of through the process so far, and really notice where you FEEL these in your body.

What colour do you associate with that emotion?

Does it have a shape?

And if you could replace that unwanted feeling with a positive emotion, what would you name that desired FEELING?

Does that emotion have a colour?

This is an important exercise as it is going to be implemented in your complimentary guided meditation, which is in your resource area, to support you moving forward on your healing journey.

https://traumaandanxietybreakthrough.com/**book-resources**/

---

*"There's No Doubt the Past Can Hurt, But We Can Either Run from It or Heal from It."*

---

## Emotional Band Aids:

Highlighting these potential issues is not done to induce shame or guilt.

The important thing to understand is that these emotional band aids are not your fault. These parts are not there with the intention of causing you more suffering or making your life harder in any way, even if the result is in fact doing that.

The emotional band aid's primary intention is to distract or soothe you away from feeling those self-belief and activation wounds we have unpicked from all the previous exercises.

These parts only act in the moment, despite that part's impact being destructive to either yourself or others. The logical part of your brain may acknowledge this, but logic cannot always influence the emotional part of the brain that is influencing these destructive behaviours.

As I go through some of the main Emotional Band Aids, I want you to firstly avoid beating yourself up; this exercise is about gaining awareness and understanding, establishing what each part thinks would happen if it wasn't there.

Will power alone cannot overcome toxic habits when these parts are protecting you from feeling a greater pain.

Intelligently, you may know certain behaviours are destructive, but because your fear centre has associated something with pleasure or security, it will always respond in the moment to soothe or protect an emotional wound. Before logic has a chance to negotiate or reason with the fear centre, permission has already been granted. This explains why you find it difficult to resist temptations when they are staring you straight in the face.

Just as you are learning to acknowledge why you behave the way that you do and look at yourself more compassionately, equally, I want you to start adopting this same approach when evaluating the responses of others towards you.

This is in no way an attempt to excuse bad behaviour - particularly when we are evaluating the behaviours of your abuser - rather, it is an explanation so you avoid the trap we can all fall into of blaming ourselves for other people's behaviour.

So, grab your notebook and start making a note of all your emotional band aids.

If there are any that I've not covered that you think could be having a negative impact on your life, get it down and go through the same series of questions.

- Ask yourself what purpose is each emotional band aid serving?
- What does your unconscious mind think would happen if that part was taken away?
- After acknowledging that parts intention, identify what the negative impact is or could be on your life directly, or that of others, if your unconscious mind continues to utilise it as a means of self-soothing.

## EMOTIONAL BAND AIDS

Some common emotions that are part of our emotional first aid box are:

**Anger**

**Being highly defensive/feeling a need to justify yourself**

These are commonly there as a way of your system giving you a sense of feeling as though somebody is supporting you and fighting your corner.

These were common emotions for me, both when I was in my abusive relationship and when going through divorce. Every time the ex would accuse me of something or make slanderous statements, it never felt enough for me to know everything he was saying were lies. I had this compulsion to constantly justify myself to people who were not asking me for an explanation.

This was my defensive part showing up in full force.

**Judgemental & Interfering in other people's issues.**

This is a distraction away from our own short comings or problems. And when it comes to trying to fix other people's problems, this potentially could lead to praise which provides us with those breadcrumbs of gratification. For a moment we feel good enough.

**Procrastination**

This part shatters so many dreams and stops us living life to our full potential.

Usually, procrastination is associated with judgement or failure.

**Denial**

Denial often shows up to protect us from feeling guilt or shame.

## Imposter syndrome

This part often shows up when we don't feel good enough or worthy enough for a particular role. You may compare yourself to others more qualified or more experienced than you.

This part makes you feel like a fraud.

## Humour

Humour, or laughing at completely inappropriate times, is an emotional part that comes up when faced with an uncomfortable situation.

## Stammering

Stammering is a nervous part, that prevents you from expressing yourself freely. This could be through fear of being judged, fear of offending someone or fear of speaking out leading to abuse.

## Addiction

Turning to Alcohol or other substances is a common crutch used to cope with day-to-day stresses. Substances are means of numbing out and forgetting about a deeper pain.

Experiencing any kind of emotional overwhelm, whether that's a result of the kids sending your head into a spin or pressures in work or business, how many catch themselves uttering:

### "I JUST NEED A GLASS OF WINE"

That isn't by accident. Your amygdala (the fear centre in the brain) has given you permission well in advance to engage in that indulgent glass of wine as a means of soothing a deeper wound.

I'm using alcohol as my primary example just because it is the most common, but the same principles apply to anyone who turns to any kind of drug to self soothe.

Maybe something has happened in the day that's activated the alarm bells and, rather than you feeling that pain, your brain is giving you permission to forget or numb it out for a little while.

Certainly, in the case of alcohol, the fear centre often associates this with pleasure. Which is why alcohol dependency is such a growing problem in society.

Society has conditioned our unconscious mind to associate this with not just socialising and having fun, but also, we as a society, associate alcohol with unwinding and relaxing after a long day.

Unfortunately, despite the good intentions of the unconscious mind, this has devastating consequences on our long-term health. In fact, due to alcohol being a mood enhancer, this actually heightens any existing low mood if the landscape isn't altered by including social engagement with friends or loved ones. Contrary to popular belief, it isn't the stimulant that makes you feel good, it is all the other things representing the landscape that provides that feel good feeling:

Dancing;

Singing;

Hugging;

Kissing;

Laughing;

Smiling.

All these promote the release of happy hormones which the drink will naturally enhance, with it being a mood enhancer. However, the minute our landscape alters, and we are left with the original encoded fears and thoughts, our emotional state defaults back to the emotional state prior to the alcohol intake. Only, dependant on the volume of alcohol in the blood, the negative emotions could now be enhanced, which could lead to suicide or self-harm.

Since Covid 19 lockdown, the number of people drinking excessively has dramatically increased, along with the number of domestic abuse cases and suicide.

This is because isolation and redundancies has shone a great big spotlight on abandonment wounds and self-belief wounds that represent inadequacy. Since the unconscious mind associates alcohol with an abundance of happy hormones, it instantly directs you to what it thinks will distract you away from feeling emotional distress. But without the presence of the true source of happiness and joy, the alcohol only enhances the emotions associated with those emotional wounds, leading to emotional breaking point.

As we covered earlier in the book, abusers are behaving the way they are due to their emotional wounds, so if they have also turned to drink during lockdown and it has enhanced their existing behaviours, this can explain one reason why domestic abuse has been on the increase since we went into covid lockdown.

Likewise, the one being abused in the home could be turning to substances to numb out and escape their internal nightmare.

The brain only ever wants to make you feel better in the moment and it will guide you to what it remembers enhancing your mood, which is why substances aren't the only thing the brain can look to as a means of making you feel better in the moment. The same applies to anything that promotes the release of dopamine. That could be food, gambling, shopping, sex, drugs, cigarettes, even exercise.

All of these things are fine to engage in as a means of soothing the soul, but when they have a destructive influence on other areas of your life, such as your health or financial security, or starts to impact or infringe on the lives and happiness of those closest to you, that's when we need to start to look within and establish what that part is keeping us from feeling.

Alcohol dependency is one issue that needs to be approached very carefully. Depending on daily consumption levels, cold turkey or reducing significantly suddenly could lead to the onset of alcoholic seizures. These can be life threatening. I talk about this when we look at lifestyle factors, but if you are concerned about the level of alcohol you are consuming daily, please contact your GP.

Really have a think about what lifestyle choices you use to self-soothe that may otherwise be having a negative impact on yours or a loved one's life. It is important to be honest with yourself about these as it is too easy to try justifying or downplaying certain behaviours because they are seen as sociably acceptable.

**Nervous Habits**

Self-harm, nail biting or other nervous habits, like pulling eyelashes or eyebrow hairs out.

Even nervously fiddling with your hair. These are all distractions from feeling something else.

Although self-harm is causing physical pain to oneself, to the unconscious mind, it is less painful than FEELING that emotional pain of not feeling good enough.

These become so involuntary, you won't even realise you are doing these things a lot of the time, resulting in the habit being the instant go-to whenever the unconscious mind is alerted to any snapshots representing danger.

**Weight Issues**

This is such a common part that affects so many people who experience trauma.

This can be for several reasons.

Firstly, as I've covered at the start of the book, cortisol plays a significant role in causing inflammation, preventing you toning or building muscle.

Additionally, the fight/flight response not only hinders the digestive process, but also affects how well we regulate our inflammatory response. When we consider Obesity is an inflammatory disorder, this becomes a big stumbling block when wanting to lose inches. The brain also holds onto fat as a means of preserving energy for the fight/flight response. Furthermore, fat can be a way of the brain protecting you from feeling a past emotion linked to an event.

**An example of this is:**

Take a woman who has experienced a miscarriage. The loss of that child is a traumatic experience. If that event is encoded as inescapable, the brain will associate certain conditions with that loss.

This is unique to everyone but potentially, the brain could associate feeling and looking attractive with intimacy. Intimacy is directly linked to pregnancy and the loss. By the brain holding onto fat, making this woman feel unattractive, the brain thinks it is protecting her from feeling that pain of the loss.

The same principle can be used with a bad breakup. This was the case for one of my case study ladies; by holding onto the inches, the brain was protecting her from feeling that pain again. Essentially, her lack of confidence in herself impacted her belief in the dating process, so instantly, she was a magnet for all the wrong men, or she simply ended up running a country mile away without giving the relationship a chance. The moment we addressed the root cause of the problem, that's when several issues started to resolve, including the stubborn inches.

You can checkout the video testimonial from Isabella on my website.

If you head on over to the resource area, I have a video training that goes a bit deeper into inch loss.

**Illness and Pain:**

Illness is another area which comes about as a result of being in our sympathetic system.

Additionally, the brain can create illness and pain as a way of distracting or taking our attention away from something it deems more painful.

I've mentioned this a couple of time now, the brain acts only in the moment, and emotion 95% of the time, overrides logic.

Intelligently, we know being ill or having pain isn't a pleasant experience, particularly if it's an illness that's potentially life threatening. To the brain that past emotional trauma is far worse. Not only do any physical symptoms move your attention away from feeling not good enough, illness and pain can also often be associated with a sense of belonging, acknowledgement, even love. If your unconscious mind identifies when you are particularly unwell you gain people's attention or love, the brain will associate the illness as serving a purpose.

Therefore, support groups for certain conditions can cause problems. Groups of people suffering the same symptoms and disease can provide a sense of safety, meaning the illness serves a greater purpose. Association and language is something we need to be careful with when experiencing any chronic illness or pain.

This is something I can relate to personally, after tracing back all my Crohn's flares to times where I've felt under pressure to achieve a level of success. Illness was a way of my brain protecting me from feeling the emotional wounds of failure. Failure meant I was ignored, making me feel worthless and unloved. That, to my system, was far too painful to bear. Illness meant that expectation from others was lifted, and I felt seen, heard, and loved, without the burden of success. The illness had a purpose.

A tool I find helpful is Louise Hay's theory to certain ailments and body parts associating with certain meaning and beliefs. It is a little WOO WOO, which I know isn't everyone's cup of tea, but for me, it certainly ties in with my story.

**Crohn's Disease:**

Fear, worry, not feeling good enough... I started with Crohn's symptoms back when I was at school, feeling all these things.

## SARCOMA IN MY KNEE

Cancer: Deep hurt, resentment, deep secret or grief eating away at the self, carrying hatred... very relevant when my Ex locked me and our daughter out:

Knee: Pride/ego, being stubborn, inability to bend, fear, won't give in.

Leg: Carry us forward in life.

Left side of body: Feminine energy, women, mother.

Muscle: Resistant to new experiences with an inability to move forward.

... for the 4 years after being locked out, I refused to accept having a broken marriage. I refused to accept my daughter having a broken home. I had this image in my head how being a mother should be, and how life should be for a woman of my age. I was very much resistant to change and continued to fight for something that was never going to change or improve.

During some of the mind games through the divorce process, I developed kidney stones and UTIs. This represents lumps of unresolved anger, pissed off - usually towards the opposite sex.

Although the Louise Hey theory may appear a bit WOO WOO, the relevance in this for me, and so many others, is on point when you compare with the beliefs and emotions you feel today and those you unpick from your time line.

**I'll add the link into the resource area if it's something you're curious about.**

I just want to elaborate a little bit more on pain before we move on.

As we have established pain can occur as a way from distracting away from something else, but pain can also be the brain's way of alerting you to a medical problem, which is why pain should never be ignored. If you experience the onset of sudden pain, always have it investigated with a medical professional.

Pain can also come about from an injury occurring at the same time as a traumatic event. A prime example of this was one used when I was doing my training...

A lady was in a taxi incident whilst in London and despite injuring her hand, she felt no pain as a result of her focus being on the conditions surrounding the accident whilst trapped.

The hand injury wasn't her focus so didn't cause any problems until she returned to London to live.

Because the injury occurred at the time of the emotional encoding, one of the event snapshots was London itself. Simply being back in the city was enough to alert the amygdala of potential danger. This directed her attention back to the hand injury and pain was experienced in the hand.

In this example, the physical pain is associated with emotional pain as a result of the emotions also being stored in the fascia of the muscle.

I experienced something very similar with my own back, when I was car jacked many years ago which resulted in a shoulder injury.

My boyfriend at the time was cheating on me with his best friend's wife. That emotional experience overlapped the physical injury when I was car jacked. After that, whenever I experienced emotional overwhelm from my ex-husband, this triggered the same emotions felt when my ex-boyfriend was cheating on me, which instantly resulted in me experiencing neck and upper back pain. The emotion was not only encoded on the fear centre, but it was also stored in the lining of the muscle.

In this instance, we must address the emotional encoding of the emotional distress, not the injury.

For this task, I'd like you to use the parts downloadable sheet in the resource area and map out which parts make up your emotional first aid box.

Get curious:

What is that parts role?

What does that part think would happen if it wasn't there for you?

What would you feel or experience that's too painful to bear if that part was removed from your life?

Thinking about that emotion the part is protecting you from:

Does that emotion have a colour?

Does it have a shape?

Where in your body do you feel these emotions?

## MORE RE PARENTING TASKS:

I have already given you some exercises throughout this section to help you identify what your emotional and self-belief wounds are, where they may have originated from, and what parts are making up your emotional tool kit.

I want you to journal these out and try to re-frame or put those parts into question.

Is there a more supporting role you can give that part?

I will use one of my own examples for you:

I felt I was a failure.

In fact, this was nailed into me by my ex-husband.

When listing and journaling all the times I have been successful, I instantly put that belief into question by providing real life examples.

My illness part:

I listed all the ways having chronic illness impacted my life negatively. More importantly, I acknowledged what me being unwell meant for my daughter who depended on me to keep her safe, happy and well.

Using the tools I guide you through in the resource area, I was able to keep that illness part in check because although its presence removes expectation, by connecting with the distress I would feel if I failed my daughter, it allowed me to negotiate with that part to support and work with me to find balance.

- Now I would like you to really think about how you, as your adult self, can start to nurture and provide that hurt little girl with everything she needed as a child.

When I say this, it may not necessarily mean re living your childhood, although if engaging in activities that filled your heart with joy as a child, you may want to introduce these back into your life.

Can you recreate any of these with your own children?

Maybe you loved to go horse riding or ice skating as a child. Is that an activity you can do either on your own or with your own children?

Make a bucket list and think about how you can start to integrate these things into your future or chill out time.

- Positive connection list

Who within your circle of friends or family has a positive impact on the way you feel?

Who leaves you feeling drained?

It is important for our emotional well-being that we spend most of our time with the people who lift us up. Schedule in time to reach out and connect with those who have a positive influence in your life and think about how you can minimise the contact with those who have the opposite effect.

- Make new connections and friendships.

Is there anyone you would like to get to know better within your circle? Reach out and connect and make new friendships with like-minded people. Are you in business or want to be in business? Connect with mums in business groups for positive social interaction.

- Set an intention daily, or a promise to yourself to do something for you. Start off small and build on those daily commitments to yourself.
- Be aware of how your environment makes you feel.

So, if the sight of mess effects your mood, what could you do to keep on top of the household jobs better?

- Pamper yourself.

Even if you can't find the time or the money to go to a salon or a spa, run yourself a bath, commit to a good skincare routine, paint your own nails, take the time to dress to make yourself feel good.

These things may seem simple but if we look good, we feel good, and when we feel good this has a knock-on effect to the rest of our day.

- Implement a good bedtime routine for yourself. Going to bed and waking up at the same time, gives the system a sense of stability, just as it would with a child. And stability and routine make the system feel safe.
- 3D Vision board.

This is a tool I came across from the beautiful Sarah Stone, who is a creative feng shui expert.

Like in traditional Feng Shui, North, East, South, and West represent different areas of our life, from travel, to finance, to love, and Sarah implements this into not just a vision board, but also inside the home.

I'm not going to go too deeply into this as Sarah is the expert on this subject, but if this is something you would like to investigate further, I will add the link to her book in the resource area. But with your own vision board, try including self-care things so you can see these things and remind yourself each day.

Also, when filling in your vision board, find pictures to reflect your self-care. Include your values on your vision board. Additional to the images, write each of these things out and stick the words to the vision board so you are accessing and activating the different parts of the brain.

- Nutrition and lifestyle.

Really think about whether your diet and lifestyle habits compliment how you want to feel. Are they in any way compromising your well-being?

I am diving deeper into this subject in the next section of the book, but as you have discovered just how much of an impact our emotional state can influence our health, it is no good fixing the mind if the mind isn't armed with the knowledge to make better choices around diet and lifestyle, which impact our health just as much.

But as we dive deeper you will start to see how it is very much a big jigsaw puzzle and one influences the other.

- And the final thing would be implementing the 5-minute rule before reacting or acting upon an urge to behave or respond in a certain way.

For example, if your amygdala has given you permission to have that glass of wine, rather than act in the moment, wait 5 minutes and ask yourself what is the purpose of that glass of wine? Is it wanting to soothe something within you? And could there be a better option that could achieve the same goal?

By allowing those 5 minutes for the active thinking brain to kick in, there is a chance logic may override emotion. This won't work with everyone, particularly when there is encoding on the amygdala, but it certainly is worth implementing and starting to train and condition the unconscious mind to consider a different approach that will provide a healthier hit of dopamine to the system.

This approach can be applied to emotional responses too. Rather than react with anger, take a step back for 5 minutes and see if you can regulate yourself so you're able to rationally think and respond.

https://traumaandanxietybreakthrough.com/book-resources/

# NUTRITION & LIFESTYLE

$\mathcal{A}$s this book is heavily focused on the brain and how it drives and influences everything from our behaviours to how optimally our body performs, I feel the best place to start is highlighting the essential nutrients for optimum brain and cognitive function and what diet and lifestyle habits impact this greatly.

- **Omega 3**

Most people identify the importance of Omega 3 in the diet, but what people don't realise is the important components in Omega 3 is DHA which is vital for cognitive function. In fact, DHA is essential for brain development in children.

EPA is another essential property in Omega 3 that supports the body in addressing inflammation in the body.

These properties are only found in fish oils, so if this isn't supplemented, you would need to be introducing oily fish such as sardines, salmon and mackerel.

However, to absorb and bind these essential properties that make up Omega 3, we must consume an additional property called ALA, which is another healthy fat found in foods such as avocados and flax seed.

Not all Omega 3 supplements contain all 3 essential properties, and Omega 3 fish oils really needs to be purchased cautiously as these properties deteriorate rapidly.

What you tend to find is, many supplement providers encapsulate fish oils as they are coming towards the end of their shelf life as a way of prolonging the shelf life of the oil.

Unfortunately, they are doing so when these essential components in the oil, EPA and DHA, have broken down, meaning regardless of taking a high mg of EPA & DHA, it's much less effective if the oil isn't consumed as fresh as possible.

- **Vitamin B1 & B12**

These are essential for brain function and energy production. The problem with all the B group Vitamins however, is that they are water soluble, which means they are not stored in the liver like non soluble vitamins so quickly get flushed out of the system.

The other hindering factor for Vitamin B1 is certain lifestyle factors deplete levels much quicker, these include:

Stress;

Alcohol;

Caffeine;

Sugar.

If you struggle with fatigue and indulge in any of the above, this would certainly be my first port of call in looking to improve Vitamin B1 levels and absorption. This would be done by initially starting off with taking 50mg of B1 (thiamine), 3 times a day, and starting to detox and reduce off alcohol, sugar and caffeine.

I am suggesting reducing as withdrawing too quickly off these things can induce some rather unpleasant symptoms and can cause additional unnecessary stress on the body by spiking cortisol levels further. As we have discussed throughout the book, managing cortisol levels is vital for so many reasons. Inducing additional physical and psychological overwhelm when withdrawing could force the brain to undo any effort to address these matters by granting permission to indulge once again as a means avoiding the heightened overwhelm. Therefore, pick one habit and reduce by either 10% a week if it's alcohol, or 1 serving/cup a day if it's sugar or caffeine.

## IMPORTANT NOTE

Please do reach out for additional support from a GP, if you are consuming high volumes of alcohol daily. A bottle of wine or the equivalent a day I feel would warrant reaching out to your GP. Reducing from high volumes of alcohol too quickly can do much more damage than raising cortisol levels. Alcohol withdrawal can induce alcoholic seizures, which are incredibly dangerous. Although the reduction plan will be as I have advised, it is essential to seek that medical advice so they can also send you for the appropriate tests to check liver and kidney function also.

- Alcohol, sugar and caffeine all contribute to the onset of inflammation also.

If weight management is a part that is showing up for you, then managing inflammation is critical to addressing this problem.

One thing not many people realise is that obesity is an inflammatory disorder, and it is a very difficult thing to get control of if any part of the health jigsaw is out of alignment. Inflammation occurs from psychological factors as we have covered.

Additionally, diet and lifestyle factors contribute to inflammation either by raising acidity levels or spiking insulin production. When inflammation is present, this then initiates the pancreas to release further insulin, which then results in further inflammation. This means the inflammatory cycle keeps repeating unless the body can regulate inflammation effectively. Therefore, the full jigsaw must be completed to break the cycle.

So, what other things influence insulin production other than sugar?

- **Carbohydrates**

We do need carbs to give us energy which is why it is important to understand the difference between the two different carbohydrates.

**Simple Carbs** are the ones to avoid because they cause the pancreas to release insulin rapidly. As our energy reserves are being topped up, if we are unable to burn off the previous reserves quick enough, this additional shot of fuel has nowhere to go, so is stored as fat!

The more insulin we release from the intake of simple carbs and sucrose (which is essentially what we know as table sugar), the more the brain craves these foods due to the ability to enhance our mood.

Even Fructose, which is fruit sugar needs to be consumed with caution. Although fruit is a healthy option, if we consume too much in one sitting it will spike insulin levels too much. One of the worst ways to consume fructose is in juice form, with the removal of the non-soluble fibre in the juicing process, it rapidly increases the absorption into the blood stream causing you to crave more.

An adult shouldn't be going much over 30g of sugar a day. Start paying attention to labels and you will see just how easy it is to exceed this.

**Complex Carbohydrates**, are broken down and absorbed at a much slower rate, meaning the pancreas doesn't release insulin quite as rapidly.

This allows our energy stores to be topped up on a slow drip process, giving the body time to burn off energy between servings. This slow release means the source of carbohydrate doesn't act as a mood enhancer, so smaller food portions and less snacking between meals is more easily achieved.

Keeping on the topic with weight management, another important nutrient and one that is often overlooked is **Protein**. Protein is essential for building and repairing muscle. If we are not maintaining lean muscle, we struggle to maintain results due to the fat metabolising process remaining sluggish.

Losing lean muscle can often lead you into a false sense of security with the scales due to muscle weighing much more than fat does. You could lose lots of weight but very little inches relative to what's showing on the scales.

The average women need to be consuming at least 50g/60g of protein a day. If you are working out this must increase to 80g/100g of protein.

### Acidic foods and drink

Raising the acidity levels in the gut significantly contributes to inflammation, which impacts the healthy cells that make up the immune system as well as damaging the gut flora.

### Antioxidants

Antioxidants are an area not many people understand. Antioxidants are essential to slow down the aging process and improve immunity.

We have two types of antioxidants.

Secondary Antioxidants, which are the dietary kind, only slow down cell damage. It is with our Primary Antioxidants where the magic happens.

Primary Antioxidants are naturally produced by the body. If you look at the pyramid bellow, the higher up the pyramid, the more responsive the antioxidant is in protecting us from free radicals produced through stress and environmental factors.

**SOD** is our front-line defence but lacks stamina.

SOD, becomes sluggish with age. The only way to improve this is to consume foods that also contain SOD so it can improve our own SOD production. The only two known sources are a special melon powder where the SOD is extracted from the cantaloupe melon. The other source is Chaga mushroom, which is a fungus that grows off the birch tree in Canada and is boiled and consumed as a tea.

**CATALASE** is what I refer to as the middle-distance runner.

This takes over from SOD as it becomes tired. Catalase is also impacted as a result of the aging process but is much easier to stimulate through more readily available foods: raw carrots, red peppers, kale, Pak choi, these all contain Catalase. But Catalase enzymes are heat sensitive, which is why I specifically state raw.

This enzyme also must be consumed super fresh to influence our natural catalase production, therefore, growing your own or buying from a local farmer is best.

**GLUTATHIONE PEROXADASE** this is much slower to respond to free radicals, therefore performs a mopping up process after SOD and Catalase has done most of the heavy lifting.

This naturally producing antioxidant however isn't affected by age, but it is affected by poor diet. Therefore, by improving your diet, you naturally improve your body's ability to prevent cell damage.

Referring to the pyramid.

The further down an antioxidant is, the slower it is to react. Therefore, typical dietary antioxidants are not as effective as people are led to believe. Vitamins and minerals are essential for their own individual reasons, but as an effective antioxidant, not so much.

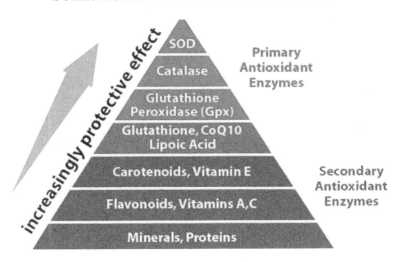

The final part of nutrition I wanted to touch on for you was **IRON** and **Vitamin C.**

Iron and Vitamin C are two nutrients that can contribute to fatigue if we become deficient in one or the other. Iron is required to produce haemoglobin, which transports oxygen from the lungs round the body. However, even if iron is being consumed adequately, if Vitamin C levels drop, iron cannot bind, which then leads to anaemia.

As I explained with the B group of vitamins being water soluble, Vitamin C also is water soluble so requires drip fed consistently through the day.

## WHAT SORT OF MEALS ARE GOING TO BEST SUPPORT YOUR HEALING?

Keeping in mind while you are going through the process of regulating your nervous system, using your tools consistently to tone your vegus nerve, keeping to foods that are easy to digest is your best choice.

Keep to foods such as chicken and fish, ideally including some of those oily fishes into your meal planning that we discussed in the Omega 3 section.

The other thing to consider is keeping some of your meals to liquid, incorporating Protein powders that are low in sugar and high nutritional value.

There are two which I recommend which I can provide the links to in your resource area.

The final thing on the nutritional side of things is intolerances and food allergies.

These can play absolute havoc with our gut health, and they are more common than we think. There is an easy and convenient way to have these tested using a hair sample test. If this is something you would like me to arrange, this can be done by post. The details for this are in your resource area with a health assessment form. You can also view a sample diagnostic report in your resource area so you can see just how detailed these are, highlighting nutritional deficiencies, severity of a food intolerance, hydration and so much more.

I've only been able to scratch the surface on the nutrition side of things in the book, but I wanted to cover some key points for you that would support you on your healing journey, both psychologically and physically, which both have a direct impact on each other.

https://traumaandanxietybreakthrough.com/book-resources/

# FLOURISHING TO A BRIGHTER FUTURE

$\mathcal{T}$his chapter is all about creating the best version of YOU!

When we come out of a domestic abusive relationship, it can be difficult to see a better future. I promise you, if you approach it in baby steps, without setting your sights too far into the future, you will make more progress than you would if you set yourself a huge goal that may feel completely out of reach.

We don't want to send our fear centre into a spin and reject any intentions that are being set.

## SLOW AND STEADY WINS THE RACE

First, I want you to go back to your list of values.

Look at the first two on the list. If this exercise has been done correctly, your first two will be essential for the rest coming into fruition.

Now ask yourself, what needs to happen to meet these values?

For me, to meet my two top values, which are maintaining my health, I certainly need time freedom. Therefore, working smarter to reach financial stability is incredibly important. Burning the candle at both ends, given my history with my health, will potentially have me taking three steps forward and two steps back.

This means getting my head out of the clouds and getting clear on how much I need to bring in from a financial perspective to live comfortably, without having to depend on outside sources.

Notice I said comfortably, not in luxury! I am setting my sights high enough to motivate me, but not so high that my system feels pressured to run before I am even off the starting blocks.

Now you have a realistic goal, how are you going to make this happen over the next 12 months?

Do you need to advance your skills? If so, can you start to explore an affordable way to get started with this?

If you have savings to invest, great, but ensure you invest wisely. Always think, is this investment going to support me in making progress?

If you already have skill sets, start to think about how you can utilise those skills to move you forward.

Plan out what you are going to do each day for the next 90 days, but check in at the end of each month to see if you are on track.

If you haven't already done your VIA Strengths test, I want you to do this exercise now.

(The link for this is in your resource area)

Using the data, I want you to look at your top five strengths. Think about how you can best put these strengths to good use to move you forward in meeting your values and goals.

Now look at your lowest scoring qualities and think how you may be able to work on these to support your progress.

Visualisation and tapping into hope are going to be your biggest motivations until you start to experience your own wins.

Have a daily ritual of using your tools and visualise your life 12 months from now!

Check in on this vision periodically through the day using the tools demonstrated in your resource area.

Set some reminders on your phone to initiate that vision through the day.

Notice how you feel as you connect with your future life, reassuring your system it is safe to feel these positive emotions.

You may even have some parts popping up around about now.

It is important to be aware of these and get curious as to what they think is going to happen?

Keep referring to your tools to give your system some gentle reassurance.

These parts are likely to be imposter syndrome and procrastination.

Incorporate a small journaling exercise on your intentions for the time scale we are working towards.

Keep your focus on a person whose journey inspires you to think,

"If they can achieve what they have after .....

There is no reason I can't achieve the same"

Draw hope from that inspiration to keep going on the days those mindset monkeys show up.

Include some of this journaling, along with some nice images, to go on your vision board so it is something you see every day.

You're just wanting snappy one liner from your journaling. No essays for your vision board.

Surround yourself with like-minded people who will bolster you up if you're lacking motivation. This could be as simple as joining a group where you are all on the same journey and have similar experiences.

**The next task I would like you to complete is a Permah profile which you can see below and downloadable in the resource area.**

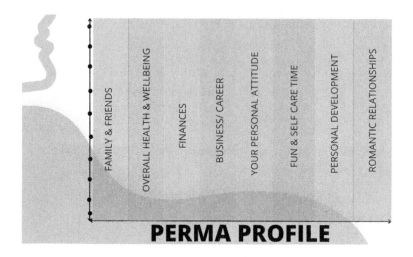

**PERMA PROFILE**

This is getting you to rate different areas of your life on a scale of 1 to 10.

10 being that you are completely satisfied with this area of your life.

What we ideally want to get to is a balance across all areas of your life.

The higher the rating on each the more fulfilled you feel. However, the likelihood is this won't be the case initially.

Think about what steps you can take to improve the areas you scored the lowest.

For example, if your friendships are leaving a lot to be desired, could you commit one night or just a couple of hours a week to spending time with family or friends.

Arrange a zoom call with a couple of your friends.

If your romantic life is lacking lustre, maybe you could sign up to a dating app when you feel ready for that step.

And one final exercise I want to cover with you is, in fact, when considering any future romantic relationships.

It is far too easy to focus on the traits and characteristics we don't want in a future partner, but it is important to focus only on the positive.

What do you want in a partner?

Get really clear on this detail and journal this out as though it is a done deal, and this person will make their way to you in divine timing.

Get clear on the things that are important to you in all relationships.

See each of these values as beautiful golden cups that ,when full, soothe your soul right to the core.

Our aim is to never feel we are compromising on what is important to us.

These Values are different to what we have done previously. Here, we are looking at things like:

LOYALTY

TRUST

TIME

PHYSICAL ATTRACTION

Obviously, if there is a good reason for one of those cups lacking in lustre due to the other person's personal circumstances, then you may look at being flexible. But if there isn't a valid or plausible reason for having to compromise one of your values, this is when we must ask: "Am I willing to settle?"

## Circle of trust

Have a review.

Who do you consider to be in your circle of trust, and who lifts you up each day?

Ensure you spend your time only with those who are going to cheer you on from the side lines and have their pom poms ready for every milestone you hit.

Spend as little time as I can with the people who are not supportive of your vision.

## Human Design

Human Design can appear very woo woo, but I really urge you to give it a go.

I'm just going to give you a basic overview of my design and how it relates so strongly to me.

I am what's known as a Projector.

Projectors see things differently to other people.

They look for ways to do things differently so they can share those gifts with the world, which is something I have always been inclined to do; in fact, I've done this with my approach to trauma.

My strategy is to be invited.

The way I should make decisions is very much through instinct. The sign that shows I am living by my design is success, and when I'm not living as my authentic self, I feel bitterness.

My strongest sense is touch. This is falls in line with my love language.

The environments I prefer are quite spaces where I can choose who I am around and who I spend my time with.

All this is very much me; I've always had a strong motivation for success, and although I connected success to a fear of failure in the past, success is still something I thrive on. If that ability to feel successful is taken from me, I can feel incredibly resentful.

Likewise, if I try to help or offer advice and that support isn't appreciated, I feel incredibly resentful.

Projectors must wait to be invited before offering advice or support.

The other thing I identified from my human design was I easily become drained if I overextend myself. I work at my best working no more than 4 hours a day. The rest of my time needs to be advancing my knowledge to share with the world.

The other types of designs are:

Specific and non-specific Manifestor

Generator

Manifesting Generator

But please do check out the link in the resource area and see what your design is.

From the free report, you will get some of the basic facts relating to your human design, but if you want to dig deeper into what the different gates mean, there are human design readers on there that can throw some light on it all for you.

I think you will have a few ah-ha moments. It may explain why your drawn to certain beliefs, feelings and values.

# YOUR JOURNEY BEYOND
# THIS BOOK

*F*irst, I really want you to give yourself a pat on the back for committing this time for yourself.

If you haven't completed all the tasks, don't beat yourself up, everybody progresses at different paces. Healing isn't a destination; it is a lifelong journey and with consistency, you will flourish and shine as the strong and confident woman you know you are.

I'm more than confident that if you consistently follow all the coaching exercises in the book, and access the resource where you have downloadable and video demonstrations to support your progress, you will build resilience.

You will build stronger foundations that will support you in moving forward to a brighter and happier future for you and your children.

I know some of you may need a bit more support throughout your healing journey or perhaps a more tailored approach.

If you would like more details on working with me further, head on over to my website to see your options.

WEBSITE: www.traumaandanxietybreakthrough.com

EMAIL: hello@traumaandanxietybreakthrough.com

If, like me, your dream is to support others suffering with the effects of trauma, I would love to invite you to join my wait list to become a Certified Practitioner in

My Trauma & Anxiety Breakthrough Formula.

Full details can be found in your resource area:

https://traumaandanxietybreakthrough.com/book-resources/

# KIND WORDS

"Kate has the innate skills of an empathic and intuitive coach. She is an effective listener and can easily recognize the root underlying issues within a presented dilemma. She quickly and thoroughly provides practical tools to help with the issue and provides accountability in a gentle but firm manner "

— TANYA B

"Kate helped me enormously in understanding my CPTSD and how to calm my mind down with strategies."

— ERICA T

"Wow thank you so much for my sessions.

I am so pleased with what we uncovered, I'm really surprised to discover that my issues all stem back from my childhood and the fear of abandonment is the reason why I have all this anxiety.

To be honest, I was extremely sceptical because nothing has ever worked in the past.

To my surprise, you DID IT!"

— JO T

"Kate is so talented and experienced in trauma.

I felt a million times better, like a big weight had been lifted off my shoulders.

Things we carry around with us without realising (a lot of baggage), a lot of it stems back to childhood and teenage years!

From doing the work with Kate, you have lightbulb moments and may explain why we acted the way we do and why "this happened".

Kate also helped my son with his dog fear and some of these techniques I was able to use with my daughter to calm her down when she is feeling anxious while out in public spaces.

Thank you Kate for all the help and support you have given me and my family"

— LOUISE CUSTARD

"My sessions with Kate have been invaluable for me.

I have experienced several breakthroughs which have amazed me.

Kate managed to access a part of my brain that I didn't know existed.

These methods have released several issues from my childhood that I didn't know were affecting me as an adult.

This has made me realise that my fear of enclosed spaces is related to some unresolved childhood issues.

Having these sessions with Kate has made me more aware of what causes my anxiety.

Therefore, I am now able to use certain tools to help me cope with any undesirable issues."

— HELEN R

"I have been working with Kate for a good couple of months now.

Kate has taken me through various techniques, ranging from hypnotherapy, havening, identifying childhood traumas etc.

The journey has been great.

Kate makes you feel relaxed and has a fantastic understanding of what therapies and tools would benefit you in your healing journey.

I still use my recordings that Kate did for me during our sessions.

They instantly make me feel so relaxed and calm.

I will keep working with Kate as I feel her in-depth knowledge and methods in various techniques are helping me tremendously"

— EMMA MARSHALL

---

"I worked with Kate last winter as I desperately wanted to get back wild swimming with my friends, but the thought of it was too much for me!

I wanted to get over my fear of the cold because sea swimming has so many benefits.

I had my sessions with Kate, and we identified my block and worked through it!

My confidence has grown, and I have now been sea swimming for many months.

I also got interviewed on a pod cast with a coaching company in the spring!

Thanks, Kate, for your immense knowledge and skills!"

— JACQUELYN HAYLEY

"I had several sessions with Kate.

After years of unresolved trauma Kate guided me through a gentle therapy that addresses the trauma, assisting me to let go and move into a more peaceful state of being.

Kate is a wealth of knowledge, she understood deeply what I was going through and had a skilful way of naturally designing every session specifically to each situation we faced together.

I watch her fb lives regularly also, which continue to encourage me on my journey.

I thoroughly recommend her services"

— HELEN MORGAN

You can check out further video feedback over on the website.

www.traumaandanxietybreakthrough.com

# ABOUT THE AUTHOR

*Photography By: Piero Belmonte Photography*

Kate is a trauma and anxiety breakthrough practitioner specialising in childhood related trauma, domestic abuse and addictions.

Kate is passionate about supporting women to break free from domestic abuse and empowering them to live a more healthy, happy and fulfilling life.

Having a young daughter, Kate understands the importance of healing our own emotional wounds to break the destructive cycle for our children.

Growing up in a toxic environment can have serious implications to a child's emotional well-being and development, which is why Kate's mission is to arm parents with trauma informed parenting tools so they can better support their children to flourish into happy and confident adults.

Kate's journey into studying the mechanics of the mind began the moment she came to the clear understanding that if she didn't break away from her abusive marriage, it could have serious implications on her own health.

Battling Crohn's disease, resulting in a perforated bowel in Oct 2018 and then overcoming a Sarcoma in her leg soon after meant living her life in a constant state of distress just wasn't an option anymore.

It wasn't an option for her, and it wasn't an option for her daughter.

Kate knew something had to change, and that change had to be her.

This is where her passion for trauma was born.

Kate prides herself on her intuitive approach, blending all the various modalities in her tool kit to achieve the absolute best results.

Kate's thirst for knowledge means she is a lifelong learner, always striving to advance her skills to better support herself and those she works with.

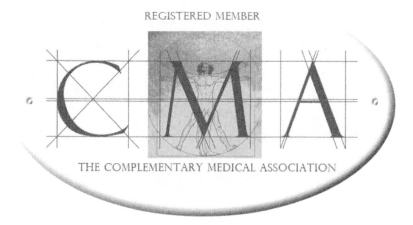

REGISTERED MEMBER

THE COMPLEMENTARY MEDICAL ASSOCIATION

**Kate's current experience and certifications include:**

Clinical Hypnotherapy,

Havening Techniques,

EMDR,

Meditation Teacher,

Children's Mindfulness,

Domestic Abuse Awareness,

PTSD Counselling and Management,

Substance Abuse Counselling,

Positive Psychology,

Advanced CBT,

Inner Child Healing.

# NOTES